Web Anatomy

Interaction Design Frameworks that Work

PRODUCT GALLERY

USER ID

PASSWORD

SIGN IN

CONTENT

Robert Hoekman, Jr.

Jared Spool

NEWS

NEWS

Web Anatomy: Interaction Design Frameworks that Work
Robert Hoekman, Jr. and Jared Spool

New Riders
1249 Eighth Street
Berkeley, CA 94710
510/524-2178
510/524-2221 (fax)

Find us on the Web at www.newriders.com
To report errors, please send a note to errata@peachpit.com
New Riders is an imprint of Peachpit, a division of Pearson Education

Acquisitions and Development Editor: Wendy Sharp
Copyeditor: Jacqueline Aaron
Production Editor: Hilal Sala
Composition: Kim Scott, Bumpy Design
Indexer: Emily Glossbrenner, FireCrystal Communications
Interior Design: Kathleen Cunningham
Cover Design: Robert Hoekman, Jr. with Mimi Heft
Cover Production: Andreas DeDanaan

ISBN-13: 978-0-321-63502-0
ISBN–10:   0-321-63502-7

9 8 7 6 5 4 3 2 1
Printed and bound in the United States of America

Acknowledgements

Robert Hoekman Jr. would like to thank the following people:

Wendy Sharp, once again, for being a great editor and friend; Jacqueline Aaron, for another superb copyediting job; Kathleen Cunningham, for a great book design; Nancy Reunzel, our esteemed publisher, for, well, being our esteemed publisher; and a whole list of other people, including but not limited to Glenn Bisignani, Nancy Davis, Gary Paul Prince, and all the other cool cats at New Riders without whom—and you knew this phrase was coming, I'm sure—this would not be possible.

I'd also, of course, like to thank my wife, Christine, who simply nodded her head and smiled as I said, for the fourth time, "God, I can't wait till I'm done with this damn book." (Writing, as it turns out, is not all glamour and roses.)

* * * * *

Jared Spool would like to thank the following people:

The amazing team at User Interface Engineering, past and present. Of particular note are the people who made all the research behind this book happen. The motto at UIE is *"Advancing Our Knowledge Through Mind-Numbing Manual Labor."* Collecting data on how people use technology takes a lot of work. Will Schroeder, Lori Landesman, Carolyn Snyder, Tara Scanlon, Nina Gilmore, Matthew Klee, Joshua Porter, and Christine Perfetti are just some of the folks who made the research come to life. Everything we reported here started with their dedication and efforts.

I'd also like to thank Wendy Sharp and the team at New Riders for putting up with my crap and their dedication to making this book into what you see. I'd also like to give a hearty thanks to my partner on this project. Robert did all the heavy lifting and deserves great credit. He's a blast to work with and (except when I was pissing him off) we had great fun!

And a special thanks go to my kids, Ari and Reed, who have been great support and inspiration, as I try to make a better world for them. Finally, Dana Chisnell should get a statue built in her honor for her support and dedication throughout this process.

*   *   *   *   *

We would together like to thank all those who came before us, doing the diligent and noble work of advocating for standards and best practices with regard to design patterns and components, including Christian Crumlish, Luke Wroblewski, Teresa Neil, Bill Scott, Martijn van Welie, Dan Brown, and Nathan Curtis of Eight Shapes, Jenifer Tidwell, and others. Without your work, the web would be a giant, disorganized mess. Well, a worse giant, disorganized mess.

Contents

PART ONE

Introducing Frameworks

PRODUCT GALLERY

USER ID

PASSWORD

SIGN IN

CONTENT

NEWS

NEWS

The Case for Frameworks

n 1998, usability expert Rolf Molich gave nine teams three weeks each to evaluate the webmail application www.hotmail.com. The experiment was part of a series of what he called Comparative Usability Evaluations (CUEs), which he began in an effort to identify a set of standards and best practices for usability tests. In each test, Rolf asked a variety of usability teams to evaluate a single design using the method of their choosing.

From the teams' documented results of one such test—called CUE-2, as it was the second test in the series—an astonishing trend appeared.

Despite claims that usability professionals operate in a scientific fashion to determine the problems within an interface, usability evaluations are, at best, less than scientific.

In an interview with Christine Perfetti (formerly of Jared's company, User Interface Engineering, or UIE) about his evaluations, Rolf said this:

> The CUE-2 teams reported 310 different usability problems. The most frequently reported problem was reported by seven of the nine teams. Only six problems were reported by more than half of the teams, while 232 problems (75 percent) were reported only once. Many of the problems that were classified as "serious" were only reported by a single team. Even the tasks used

by most or all teams produced very different results—around 70 percent of the findings for each of these common tasks were unique.

In CUE-4 (http://www.dialogdesign.dk/Summary3.htm), run in 2003, a total of seventeen teams were hired to evaluate www.hotelpenn.com, which featured a Flash-based reservation system developed by iHotelier. Of the seventeen teams, nine ran usability tests, and the remaining eight performed expert reviews.

Collectively, the teams reported 340 usability issues. However, only nine of these issues were reported by more than half of the teams. And a total of 205 issues—sixty percent of all the findings reported—were identified *only one time.* Sixty-one of these issues were identified as "serious" or "critical" problems.

Think about that for a moment.

In order for the Hotmail team to identify all of the "serious" usability issues brought out by the evaluation process, it would have to have hired *all nine usability teams.* In CUE-4, to spot all sixty-one serious issues, the Hotel Penn team would have to have hired seventeen usability teams. *Seventeen!*

Asked how development teams could be confident they are addressing the right problems on their websites, Rolf concluded,

It's very simple: They can't be sure!

Asked if he felt usability testing would play a major role in creating usable websites in the future, Rolf went on to explain,

[We] should use them mainly in an intermediate phase to establish trust with our colleagues, and then use much more cost-efficient preventive methods such as usable interface building blocks, reviews based on standards and proven guidelines, and contextual inquiry.

We think Rolf's answer was incomplete. First, although usability testing is perhaps no more accurate or reliable than an expert or heuristic evaluation performed by a lone reviewer when it comes to determining whether or not you're focusing on the most significant problems—the problems whose solutions will reap the biggest benefits for the effort put into solving them—usability testing can and does offer incredibly useful insights about how people interact online, and should still very much be considered an essential tool.

Second, any evaluation or discovery method must be put in context. Page views and time-spent-per-page metrics, while once considered standard measures of site effectiveness, are meaningless until they are considered in context of the goals of the pages being visited. Is a user who visits a series of pages doing so because the task flow is effective, or because he can't find the content he is seeking? Are users spending a lot of time on a page because they're engaged, or because they're stuck? While NYTimes.com surely hopes readers will stay on a page long enough to read an article in full or scan all its headlines, Google's goal is for users to find what they need and leave a search-results page as quickly as possible. A lengthy time-spent metric on NYTimes.com could be indicative of a high-quality article. On Google.com, it could indicate a team's utter failure.

Regardless, usability evaluations can't tell designers how to design well; they can only help identify problems in designs already created. It's on this point that Rolf's next statement really resonates:

> *I hope that we will one day have huge libraries of generic interface building blocks that are thoroughly tested with real users and proven usable. I also hope that we will show how assembling such building blocks into full-blown websites by usability-conscious specialists will yield websites with a high degree of usability.*

Huge libraries. Building blocks. Thoroughly tested.

If you're wondering what Rolf's story has to do with the book you now hold in your hands, those words contain the answer. This is a book about those building blocks. Not principles. Not concepts. Not code. *Building blocks.*

The first goal of *Web Anatomy: Interaction Design Frameworks That Work* is to take a close look at these building blocks—to identify them, take them apart, and diagnose what they do and why they work—so that we, as designers, can start "assembling [them] into full-blown websites" that yield "a high degree of usability."

But that's just the first goal. We have several more. Specifically, we hope *Web Anatomy* will solve three types of problems that seem to reappear during every web project.

First, the task of translating a high-level understanding of an application's goals into low-level design details can be brutal, like trying to turn a vapor cloud into a brick wall with one hand tied behind your back and the other one lacking a magic wand. Figuring out where to start can be the most difficult step in the entire process, and even when you think you've got it all sussed out, it's hard to know you're not missing something crucial. How can you be sure you're truly meeting user needs when you're busy supporting business goals?

Second is the problem of standards versus innovation. Too often, *standard* means *boring*. We can probably all agree that the best part of any design project is devising a solution nobody has previously thought up. These moments are exhilarating—they get the heart pumping and the adrenaline flowing. But on most projects, these moments are few and far between. That's because even in the most innovative projects, the portion that counts as never-been-tried-before is only maybe twenty percent of the project. The remainder is standard support functionality. This work doesn't get the heart pumping or the adrenaline flowing—it's just nose-to-the-grindstone, must-do work that is part of every project. As such, we tend to neglect it.

Somewhere, right now, there's a team creating a new design that includes some amazing, never-before-seen functionality. But to take advantage of that groundbreaking work, users will need to sign in.

Sign-in functionality isn't new, it's not exciting, it's not very challenging to develop, and teams repeatedly have to design this functionality as if it has never been built before. This makes the tedious work of designing yet another sign-in interaction quite dull, but ignoring this work leaves the team open to big problems. Because it's not the sexy part of a project, it's likely to get neglected; this can result in an unusable and frustrating experience for users, and can cost an organization revenue.

On the flip side of this, innovation can be a problem as well. If you've been focused on designing usable interfaces for a while, you may have noticed the same thing we have: usability and innovation too often appear mutually exclusive. *Cool* and *usable* can make for terrible bedfellows.

Live.com suffered from this problem during its first release, which included the controversial **infinite scroll** design pattern. The approach was meant to eliminate the problem of forcing users to wait for new pages to load whenever they wished to go beyond the initial result set, instead loading them all into a single page as users moved through them. The reality, however, was quite different. Users, who were entirely unfamiliar with this shift in paradigm, easily became frustrated when they could never seem to reach the end of a results page and quickly dismissed the idea because, frankly, the site didn't behave like Google. While infinite scrolling may have been *cool*, it was remarkably confusing for users and therefore completely ineffective. (See Chapter 4 for more details from this story.)

In our desire to make waves in the market, we need to create brilliant interfaces, but we need to do this without sacrificing ease of use, and doing this well can be incredibly difficult. When we break away from standards, we risk designing interfaces that our users simply don't understand. Frameworks give us a way to standardize the boring support functionality so that we can spend less time *reinventing* and more time *inventing*.

Finally, there's the problem of doing more with less. Web teams are getting smaller—many are half the size they were ten years ago—but organizations are expecting more and more from each team. At the same time, projects are more sophisticated than ever. To save time and energy, teams now have to think about using what's been done before. As we said, teams constantly have to design sign-in functionality as if it has never been built before. But it *has* been built before—teams all over the world have built sign-in interaction into their applications a million times—and yet there they are, doing it all over again. All this re-creation and reinvention is remarkably inefficient. To reduce the effort required for that work (and make it possible to spend more time on the fun, exciting innovative parts), teams need designs they can reuse.

Reuse is the new priority.

Reuse Strategy

At the core of the solution to *all* of the problems we've described thus far is that very simple idea. Web teams, more and more every day, need to develop solid reuse strategies.

Reuse strategies divide into three types of libraries: patterns, components, and interaction design frameworks. These libraries can give a team speed and efficiency by letting them leverage the rich history of things implemented before.

We've found that teams that build out a reuse strategy see tangible benefits. First, they can quickly kick off their design process by starting with a collection of work that is, at its most basic level anyway, already done and can be quickly pieced together into the beginnings of a working design. These teams are also more likely to complete a design in less time, even with all the nuances and details that make for a great user experience. Next, their designs are more likely to have a high degree of usability and behave consistently across the entire set of functionality despite their having devoted less time on the relatively unexciting support functionality. Finally, the teams iterate more quickly, giving them a chance to play with the design while it's still malleable.

Patterns, components, and interaction design frameworks each play a different, essential role in a team's reuse strategy. In the next chapter, we'll take a close look at each of these library types, but first, a brief introduction.

Patterns: a catalog of desired behaviors

Inspired by the architectural patterns of Christopher Alexander, which he wrote about in the 1977 book *A Pattern Language: Towns, Building, Construction* (Oxford University Press), design patterns were the first piece of the reuse puzzle. Alexander looked at the specific behaviors of how people lived and worked, and created reusable descriptions of how a building's architecture could support those behaviors. The pattern didn't lock architects into cookie-cutter designs, but instead gave them a resource to ensure they got all the details right.

Today's design patterns are similar. For example, let's say a user needs to enter a date while booking a reservation. What are the different designs that could support entering a date? A free-form text box with a parser? Three numeric tumblers, representing month, day, and year? A calendar pop-up, where the user just points and clicks?

Each option represents a design response to the same behavior. When the team specifies the response that works best for them (and their users), they can codify it in a pattern. Future teams, needing to respond to that desired behavior, can now respond similarly, meeting established user expectations while leveraging the previous work.

Figure 1.1
A pattern document
from the Yahoo Design
Pattern Library

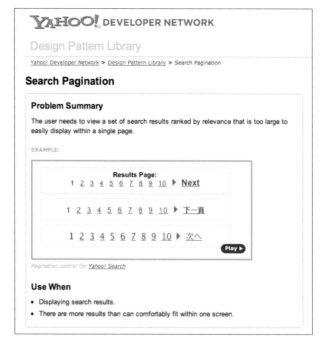

Components: taking advantage of reusable code

Beyond patterns, however, developers needed an easy way to reuse specific code.

Once we choose which pattern to use, it's time to consider its implementation. For a pop-up calendar to work, dates have to appear on the screen. The calendar has to respond to the mouse clicks. It needs to look like it is part of the rest of the application. This is where components come in.

Components specify the design response at the *pixel*-level. Because they often are represented by their code, components embody specific interaction behavior. They are functioning design solutions complete with styling elements such as fonts, colors, and layout.

Developers use components to piece together the specifics of a design. Once built, they are ready-made elements that can be easily plugged into any new screen. This speeds every part of the development process, from early prototypes to final deployment. In short, a component is a code-complete, modularized, and implementable version of a design pattern.

Figure 1.2
Component
documentation, as
presented on Sun.com

Frameworks: the final puzzle piece

The interaction design framework—the subject of this book—is the newest member of the trinity. Whereas a design pattern is a common solution to a recurring problem, an interaction design framework is a *set* of design patterns plus other elements and information, used together to guide the design of a complete system or site context.

Like the human body, every web app is made up of a group of anatomical systems that work together to create the larger whole. And each system contains a collection of individual parts, each with its own purpose and function. If we take a close look at the anatomy of successful (and unsuccessful) websites and applications, we can not only identify the elements that are most typically used to meet user needs in a variety of contexts, but also learn quite a bit about human behavior to improve upon these standards and take our designs to the next level without sacrificing usability.

Figure 1.3
A framework document

In other words, if we simply look at what's already working well, and *why*, we can give ourselves a solution to both problems: a starting point for the design, and insight into how to create better-stronger-faster interactions that are just as easy to use as the old classics.

For example, in Chapter 4, we describe that a **sign-up framework** is composed of several design elements all typically used to encourage users to sign up for an application. Each element can, by itself, be considered a design pattern. The **elevator pitch**, for example (a short statement about the app's value proposition), is used to quickly and efficiently let people know what a site or an application might offer—but although an elevator pitch answers a question in the user's mind and therefore solves a problem, it's not a very meaningful problem. Rather, it's part of a much larger problem—the problem of how to convince people to sign up for your shiny new web application.

Rather than supply a narrow solution to a narrow problem, a framework handles more complex problems. It offers guidelines for the design of *whole contexts*.

When a user arrives at a new site and is trying to figure out whether or not to sign up, the sign-up framework makes a clear pitch, answers questions, offers a way to get started, and provides a way to register. No single design pattern can handle all this. It's the *combination* of these elements that really solves the problem. Further, no single design pattern can tell us how to meet all these user needs, nor can it tell us why they need to be handled in the first place.

To fill this void, frameworks describe entire subsystems of patterns. A sign-in subsystem needs a pattern where users enter an ID and password. But it also needs a pattern for password recovery, a pattern for setting up the ID initially, a pattern for creating new IDs, and a pattern for changing the password.

Teams identify and document frameworks by looking at other designs and extracting their commonalities. These elements become a checklist for a complete system, helping the team ensure they have all the right patterns to start their design.

Frameworks are at a high level of abstraction. They don't speak to specific branding or visual design requirements—that's filled in by components, which are, in turn, based on individual design patterns. Rather, frameworks are the larger anatomical systems that help designers choose which patterns to use in the first place. These anatomical systems, we believe, in conjunction with patterns and components, are Rolf's building blocks.

Pushing beyond standards

Beyond providing an effective means by which to iterate quickly and produce usable designs, however, frameworks also offer insight into the rationale behind existing standards. Through an anatomical lens, designers can reverse-engineer the logic that led to such design decisions in the first place, and can then use these insights as principles on which to base new, more innovative designs. We'll talk about this aspect of frameworks and much more in Chapter 2.

Distributing the workload

The benefits of reuse, it should be noted, don't come for free. Identifying reusable elements takes time and practice, documenting the elements can be time-consuming, and keeping the libraries up-to-date is an ongoing and demanding task.

Turning this into a trinity of patterns, components, and frameworks helps, however, because the work can then be distributed between the designers and the developers.

Because components are close to the final implementation, it's common that development team members manage this library. Meanwhile, since interaction design frameworks focus on the larger experience, we expect to see design team members take charge here. The pattern library is often a joint venture between design and development.

While small organizations can keep the library up-to-date with minimal effort, larger organizations should expect to need a significant curation effort. Its curators need to encourage team members to identify new elements for the library and perhaps add to it directly, while making sure existing elements are kept current. Since the libraries are a shared resource, the entire team shares the responsibility for the curation. This division of labor prevents any one person from carrying the burden of keeping the libraries useful. It also has the side benefit of keeping the libraries ever-present in the work life of the team members, reminding them of their availability.

Once built out, these libraries can become a powerful resource for design teams. They can inform the design process, speed delivery, and make good design the path of least resistance. The long-term cost savings from a reuse strategy more than compensates for the initial investment of developing one.

Together, these three libraries constitute what we call *The Reuse Trinity*. In the next chapter, we'll describe all three in depth and look at their relationship to each other before diving into several major frameworks to shed light on how they came to be.

New answers to old problems

By looking at the web as a collection of anatomical systems and identifying the ones that relate to your own projects, it's possible not only to jump-start your design process, but also to glean the insights you need to devise cutting-edge solutions that still work well for users, do more with fewer resources, finish projects in less time, and ensure that designs are usable from the very beginning.

Through frameworks, we get clear guidelines based on current standards. We also get a better way to see the possibilities and start putting together superior user experiences. What we don't get is a list of one-size-fits-all rules.

In other words, interaction design frameworks are just that. Frameworks. They serve as guidelines for the design of systems and contexts. They can be seamlessly strung together into complete solutions. They can (and should) be adapted, stylized, customized. They compose the building blocks of a usable design. But best of all, they can tell us how to *evolve*.

Questions, answers, and inspiration

As we worked on this book, Robert spoke about interaction design frameworks several times in workshops and conference sessions. During these sessions, Robert took note of the questions audience members and workshop attendees asked, and based on these questions, we progressively altered the content and structure of the book to address these points. Instead of simply delivering a reference book of frameworks, we felt it would be vital to very clearly communicate why they're important, what comprises them and why, what to consider when using frameworks in your own design projects, how to identify and share frameworks, how to document them, how to fit them into your design process, and how to make full use of their potential for informing innovation.

So in this book, we start by taking a close-up look at patterns, components, and frameworks and how they work together to form a complete reuse strategy. Then we examine several significant frameworks with the goal of revealing their history and effectiveness, as well as teaching you how to dissect the web in this new fashion and glean important insights on how these frameworks became standard and what can be learned from them. Next, we show you how to complete a project using frameworks, highlighting the adjustments you can make to your process to take full advantage of these new resources. Finally, we show you how to identify and start using frameworks within your own organization.

With any luck, by the end of this book we'll inspire you to start your own huge library of thoroughly tested interface building blocks.

The Reuse Trinity

I n this chapter, we take a close look at each of the three parts of the reuse so that, throughout the rest of the book, you can better see how design patterns, components, and interaction design frameworks relate to each other and work together.

The Reuse Trinity didn't come easily, nor did it develop in an entirely logical order. The notion of patterns began way back with Christopher Alexander's book in 1977, and has since been propagated by pattern advocates such as Luke Wroblewski, Bill Scott, Martijn van Welie, Teresa Neil, Christian Crumlish, Jenifer Tidwell, and many other industry experts whose hard work has brought patterns to the forefront of web design practices. Components—fully fleshed-out, production-ready page elements that represent the natural evolution of patterns—came much later, at least in terms of software design (as opposed to development).

In fact, components have only just begun to become standardized as a concept, thanks largely to the work of EightShapes designers Nathan Curtis (author of *Modular Web Design: Creating Reusable Components for User Experience Design and Documentation* (New Riders)) and Dan Brown (author of *Communicating Design: Developing Web Site Documentation for Design and Planning* (New Riders)), though less formalized variations of the idea have been around for years. Frameworks are the last to fill out the picture, and are being documented for the very first time in the book you now hold in your hands. In practical terms, however, frameworks should have come first, patterns second, and components third. This is how they can be most effectively used and thought about within a web design process.

Figure 2.1
Diagram of the Reuse
Trinity

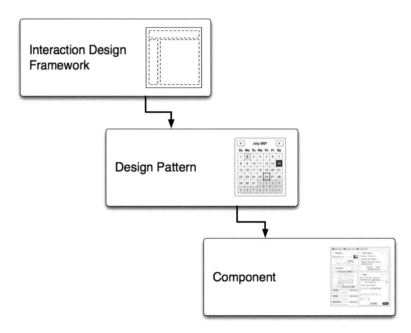

Design patterns are essentially production patterns that are part of larger frameworks, while components are the realization of patterns within the scope of a specific system, bringing patterns to the point where they can be interacted with online as a finished piece of a site or application screen.

As we go through each of these elements in some depth in this chapter, we'll do so in the order in which they were conceived. Regardless of whether or not you're already familiar with patterns and components, it will perhaps be easier to understand the big picture of frameworks with a basic understanding of the parts that comprise them.

Design Patterns

A **design pattern**, if you don't already know, is *a common solution to a common problem*. For example, the *pagination* pattern gives us a standard interface for spreading search results across multiple pages simply by adding paginated links to the bottom of each results page. The design typically includes Previous and Next buttons, numbered links that provide access to each of the next several results pages, and some sort of visual indication of the current page.

Sound familiar? It should. It's at the bottom of every Yahoo–search-results page.

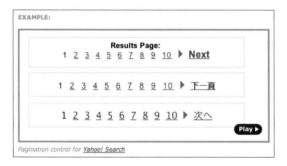

Figure 2.2
Examples of pagination interfaces from the Yahoo Design Pattern Library

Yahoo may not have been the first to use the design, but Yahoo's version is used so frequently that virtually every other search system out there features a variation of it. This makes it a pattern—a hugely successful pattern, in fact, that has been documented in countless pattern libraries, both public and private.

The primary benefit of design patterns is that they enable users to parlay their experiences from all across the web into working knowledge of any site that uses the same patterns. After using Yahoo to run a few searches, a user can easily understand the pagination interface of any other site using a similar design.

On the flip side, designers benefit greatly because patterns offer what are essentially canned solutions to a host of typical design problems. Instead of rethinking and reinventing search navigation for every new site, we can simply pull out the pagination pattern, make a few tweaks, and move on.

For years, many considered design patterns to be the building blocks of the web—for good reason—and with frameworks, we hope to build on the success of patterns.

Elements of a design pattern

To understand patterns better, let's consider what goes into a typical design-pattern description. Jared's company, UIE, turned up quite a few common elements:

Figure 2.3
A pattern document from Welie.com's public pattern library

Pattern name

If we were talking about an element to log a user into the password-protected portion of a site, we might name it "Username and Password Widget," "Two-Line Sign-in Elements," or "Log-in Element."

It's important to choose the pattern name carefully. Traditionally, many elements appear in designs without having a name, leading to discussions that contain statements like, "You know, those little box thingies we always have on the left." The goal of the pattern name is to encourage clear communication in meetings, design documents, and other places where people may want to call out a particular element.

We've seen that naming a pattern takes skill, creativity, and a little bit of luck. Teams may start out with one name, only to find later another name has become the common parlance.

For example, one team officially named its application's object attribute editor the "Infobox," only to find that nobody on the team ever referred to it that way. Instead, they all called it "Properties."

Some teams add a list of nicknames, synonyms, and also-known-as (aka) names to a pattern's description. This helps team members know what they're talking about. What we call things changes over time, so it's helpful to keep the pattern name updated to reflect the current lexicon.

Description

A description is essential for a good pattern. It helps team members who may be unfamiliar with the element to know exactly what is being talked about.

And since a picture is worth a thousand words, screen shots can also be very valuable. When a given pattern has different manifestations within a single site, multiple images can help.

A log-in element, for example, might have this description (along with appropriate screen shots):

> *A two-line form component we use to collect the user's user ID and password, so they can gain access to the password-protected portions of the website.*

A description doesn't have to be a major literary work, but it should include enough information to explain why the element exists and how to distinguish it from other elements on the site.

Context of use

One of the key benefits of a design pattern over a style guide or guideline document is the heavy emphasis on each element's context of use in a pattern library. Designers, when considering a new design, use the context description to determine if a particular pattern is appropriate.

For example, the context for our log-in element might say something like this:

> *We use this whenever a user might wish to transition from the public-facing portion of the site to access their private information. This pattern can appear on public-facing sites when there is enough real estate for a 155-pixel–by–210-pixel block.*

Of course, this section needs to include something about the log-in element when it's not used:

> *On public-facing pages where there isn't available vertical space, we use the Single-Line Log-in element in the banner bar,* or *We don't use a log-in element on pages in the password-protected portion of the site.*

Contexts are living creatures. As a team builds more elements, develops new applications, and discovers new user requirements, the Context of Use section requires frequent updates. Ideally, at any point in the pattern's lifetime, a designer can read through this section and immediately know whether or not the element is right for the job at hand.

Where used

Another living portion of the document, the Where Used section, points to instances of the pattern in use and is updated every time the pattern makes it into a production system. Team members can look at existing implementations of the pattern and see it in action.

How it works

Here, teams describe the mechanics of the element:

> *Users enter their user ID into the type-in box labeled User Name. They enter their passwords into the type-in box labeled Password (which obscures what they type). If they choose, they can click the Remember Me check box, which pre-fills the User Name field on repeat visits. When ready, the user presses the button labeled Log in. If the user name and password are valid, the*

user's personal page is displayed. If not, an error message is displayed. (See the Log-in Error pattern.)

The amount of detail necessary depends on the complexity of the control and the familiarity team members have with it. (If it's an element they personally use all the time, it probably doesn't need as much description as one they rarely encounter on their own.) One usability team showed us how they use a video-capture utility to create short demonstration videos of the elements in action, which they reference in this section.

Mentioning other patterns that interact with this one helps the designers understand what else they'll need to consider when they are putting their design together.

Co-requisites

It's rare that a pattern stands alone. The presence of one pattern usually indicates that the designer will need other patterns to support it.

For example, if a design requires the log-in element pattern, then it will likely also need the following:

- A pattern for creating a new user ID
- A pattern for changing the password
- A pattern for recovering a lost password
- A pattern to log out of the password-protected portion of the site
- A pattern to display an error message when the wrong user-name/ password combination is entered

All of these patterns are listed in the Co-requisites section along with any explanations as to why they might be required (if it's not obvious).

Design-pattern documentation can also include sections on competitive approaches, pattern history, usability test results, user feedback, and discussion.

Pattern libraries

Pattern libraries, as shown in **Figure 2.4,** are curated collections of pattern documents, often categorized and made available either online or privately within an organization.

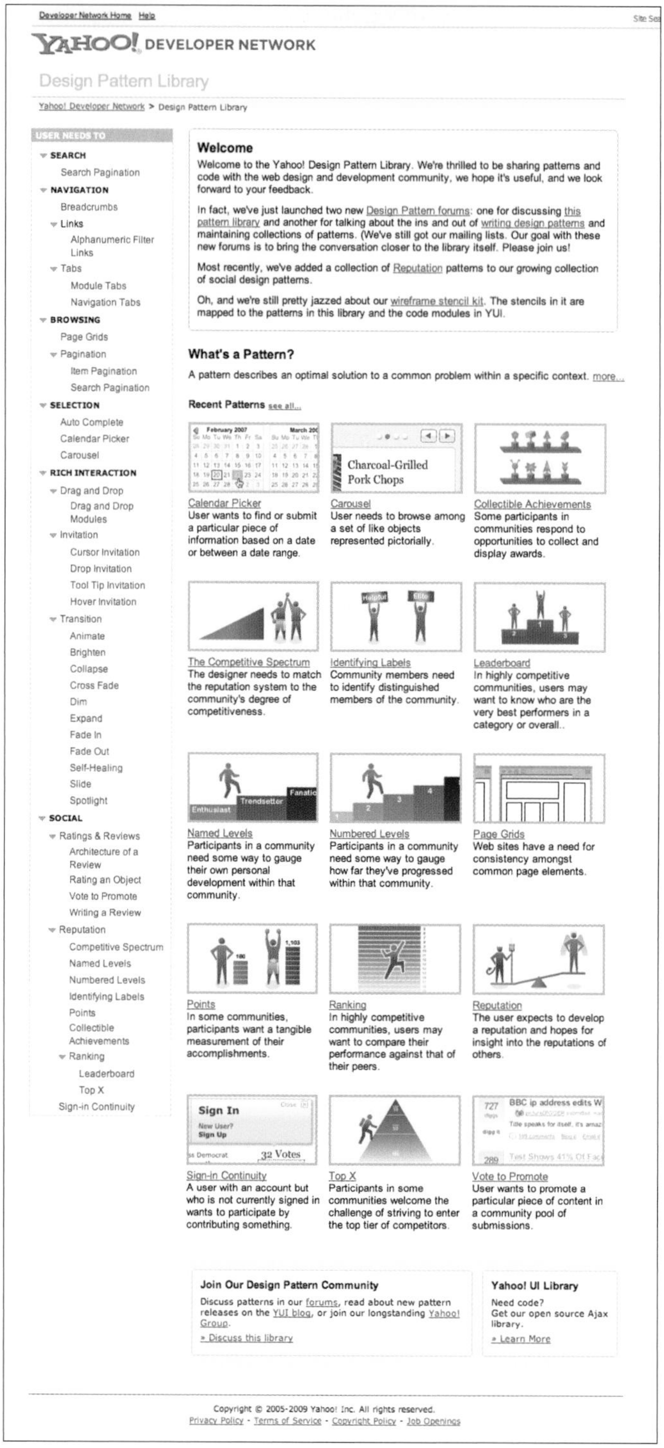

Figure 2.4
The Yahoo Design Pattern Library, one of the most popular public libraries

Here is a list of resources for several public pattern libraries:

- Yahoo Design Pattern Library: http://developer.yahoo.com/ypatterns

- Designing Interfaces (the support site for the book of the same name, by Jennifer Tidwell, published by O'Reilly): http://designinginterfaces.com

- Welie.com: http://www.welie.com

To start leveraging patterns, many teams turn to one of these off-the-shelf, public pattern libraries, but while these are often well-documented and free, they can't account for a project's specific technological constraints and business requirements, so they may be less useful for a specific project. The most helpful pattern libraries make project-specific constraints and requirements their focus.

Public pattern libraries tend to offer generic patterns—ones not specific to a given application. While they do offer low-level baseline recommendations for what are considered standard web interactions, organizations frequently individualize these patterns in their applications and sites, rendering the patterns found in public libraries too generic to be truly useful for their design teams.

That said, these generic patterns can still give great benefits. In addition to providing baseline recommendations that can serve as a great jumping-off point for the creation of customized patterns, these libraries are a fantastic resource for solo designers, either working inside an organization or consulting from outside. Since consultants tend to work on a wide range of projects for a variety of clients, public pattern libraries offer an endless supply of solutions that can be applied across many different site designs.

Internal pattern libraries, on the other hand, typically present pattern variations more specific to an organization's sites, making them a powerful tool for design teams. The team can curate their library using a wiki or microsite on their intranet, and they can tie it to their internal style guide so other teams within the organization can take advantage of the library when implementing new designs.

The major difficulty in developing a pattern library is coordinating its launch. First, individuals or teams need to sniff out patterns already in use by an organization by identifying all the instances of their use. They then need to establish a system for posting and sharing them, document each pattern, form a plan for maintaining the library in the long term, and finally, promote the library. This is no small task for a team, whose core mission is usually to meet the deadlines of much higher-priority customer-facing projects. But the payoff of a pattern library far exceeds the effort required to launch it. A team can immediately begin pointing developers to the library to answer questions about how certain interactions should look and function. And with this core piece of the reuse strategy in place, designers can spend less time reinventing what are already common solutions and spend more time on a project's unique challenges.

Components

Perhaps the simplest way to introduce components is to quote a page from the website of perhaps their most ardent advocate, the company EightShapes (http://unify.eightshapes.com/users-guide/what-you-get/wireframe-components/):

> *A component is a chunk of a page design.*
>
> *A component contains generic, atomic elements (like text, links, buttons, check boxes, and images) combined into a meaningful building block used— and reused—in your interface design of an entire page. Other common terms you may have heard to describe a page chunk include module, portlet, widget, or even molecule.*

And to paraphrase Nathan Curtis' presentation, "Creating a Component Library":

Whereas a view is a complete page or page state, and an element is something on a page that can't be broken down any further—such as a logo, header image, or button—a component is a combination of elements that creates a purposeful, reusable, and independent structure. A tabbed navigation interface. Search results. Article content.

While a pattern is a generic solution that works across sites, a component is specific to a site—very specific, in fact. While patterns are best for interaction designers and anyone else hashing out a solution using sketches, wireframes, or other low-level artifacts, components are aimed at the people who build out those designs. They're code-complete and reusable. A developer can simply plug a component into a page (and multiple components can be derived from a single pattern), customize its content, and have a completed page area.

Elements of a component

As component libraries are not yet popular enough to survey a wide variety of resources and extrapolate a set of best practices, we pulled the following list of elements from the public component library available through the Sun Microsystems website (more on this in the Component Libraries section).

Component name

The component's name, at least in the Sun library, is offered via the page title. As in pattern libraries, however, you can include a more explicit Component Name section that offers a list of alternative names used within your organization.

Component version number

Adjacent to both the component name and the heading for the Sample section (described below) is the component's version number. Like release notes for any software update, the version number can be tied to a list of changes that have occurred from one version to the next. This can help get the attention of developers who need to update previous implementations, and help teams maintain consistency across systems.

Definition

A component's Definition section, much like a pattern's Description section, simply describes the purpose of the component. In **Figure 2.5**, the definition of the B01 Features component is explained as follows:

> *The homepage feature is a complex and important part of the sun.com homepage. It displays the rotating main features and serves as a container for the 3 homepage promos.*

Figure 2.5
A Sun.com component
document

Usage

The Usage section describes where the component is to be used, and includes any relevant notes. You'll find this on Sun's D05 Primary Index Nav page:

> *Use on any index page. Use of the "See All" link is optional if there is no additional content to view.*

While the component is limited to index pages, it can be implemented in one of two ways: with and without the See All link. The Usage section simply details both of these points.

Sample

The Sample section offers a living, breathing version of the component. Since components are completed page elements, you can add fully functioning versions of them to their web-based documentation. This helps people throughout an organization see exactly how the component is meant to work (which, among other things, can help quality assurance teams verify the correctness of implemented versions), how it looks, and what code should be used to implement it.

Code

Along with a functioning sample, component documents should include a Code section that links to implemented versions of the component, created using various programming languages. If an organization has created one application with Ruby on Rails and another with Apple's Cocoa, and the component can be used in both, then the Code section should include versions created with both languages.

Component libraries

Component libraries can be developed and distributed the same way pattern libraries are—by setting up a wiki, identifying finished instances of components, and documenting them.

The Sun Microsystems website, as shown in **Figure 2.6**, includes a public component library that can easily be used as a reference for how components are documented. You can find this library at www.sun.com/webdesign.

Most usefully, Sun offers a page about how to use components (http://www.sun.com/webdesign/structuring-pages.html); the page visually describes the different sections of a standard Sun content page template. It also offers an example of a page built using the company's components (http://www.sun.com/software/products/mysql/index.jsp).

Additionally, Nathan Curtis has posted his slides, "Creating a Component Library," to SlideShare.net. It's available at http://www.slideshare.net/nathanacurtis/creating-a-component-library-298610.

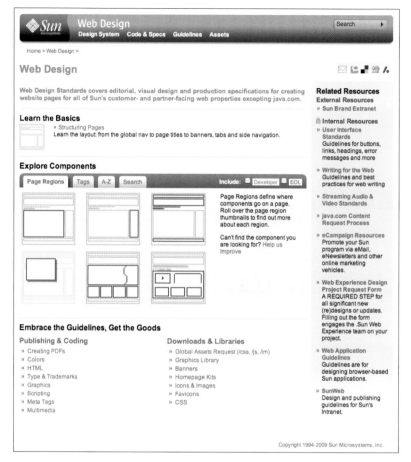

Interaction Design Frameworks

In all, there are perhaps millions of design patterns in use every day on the web—some more prevalent than others—and as such, they are ideal candidates to be called the building blocks of the web. But they also have a very important limitation.

Design patterns solve small and specific problems—exactly what we need them to do—but they don't tell us how those problems relate to and affect our solutions to other problems. Even the Context of Use section in the typical pattern document discusses only where a pattern fits into an application, not how it affects the application or how it relates to the rest of that system. And although the Co-requisites section lists other patterns that should be used in tandem, the list fails to illuminate the why behind the what.

Design patterns lack much of the contextual information we need to create a successful design, so they leave us with a lot of unanswered questions. How many search results do we show on each page? How do we handle errors (typos, zero-result searches, and the like)? How will users run new searches? How much information should be offered in each result? Which information is important? Patterns don't answers these questions.

For example, while a pagination interface enables a user to navigate from one page to the next and back again, it solves exactly one problem. It supports exactly one action. But there's much more to consider in the pursuit of usable designs.

To answer these questions, we can't look only at the pagination interface. We have to look at the whole search system. By extension, we can't rely exclusively on design patterns—we have to look at how the patterns make up systems, and how systems make up whole applications.

And since components are essentially the code-complete versions of an organization's patterns, they can't be used to answer these questions either.

To answer these questions, then, we need to look at the level above design patterns in the Reuse Trinity: interaction design frameworks.

Elements of an interaction design framework

Frameworks are structured similarly to design patterns. In fact, we consider frameworks to be the next logical evolution of design patterns—the next step in establishing a set of mature solutions. The frameworks we present in this book are exactly what we recommend you use in your own frameworks—names, descriptions, explanations of where and how they're used, and so on. Simply, each framework includes some or all of the divisions we identify in this section.

Beyond this, we also discuss the user needs these frameworks meet and the human behaviors that led to them, and we explore how these design problems could be solved differently. We've done this to provide insight into what to consider when applying frameworks to your own projects and how to make full use of the design criteria you pull out of them.

Figure 2.7
The sign-up framework document from http://webanatomy.rhjr.net/signup

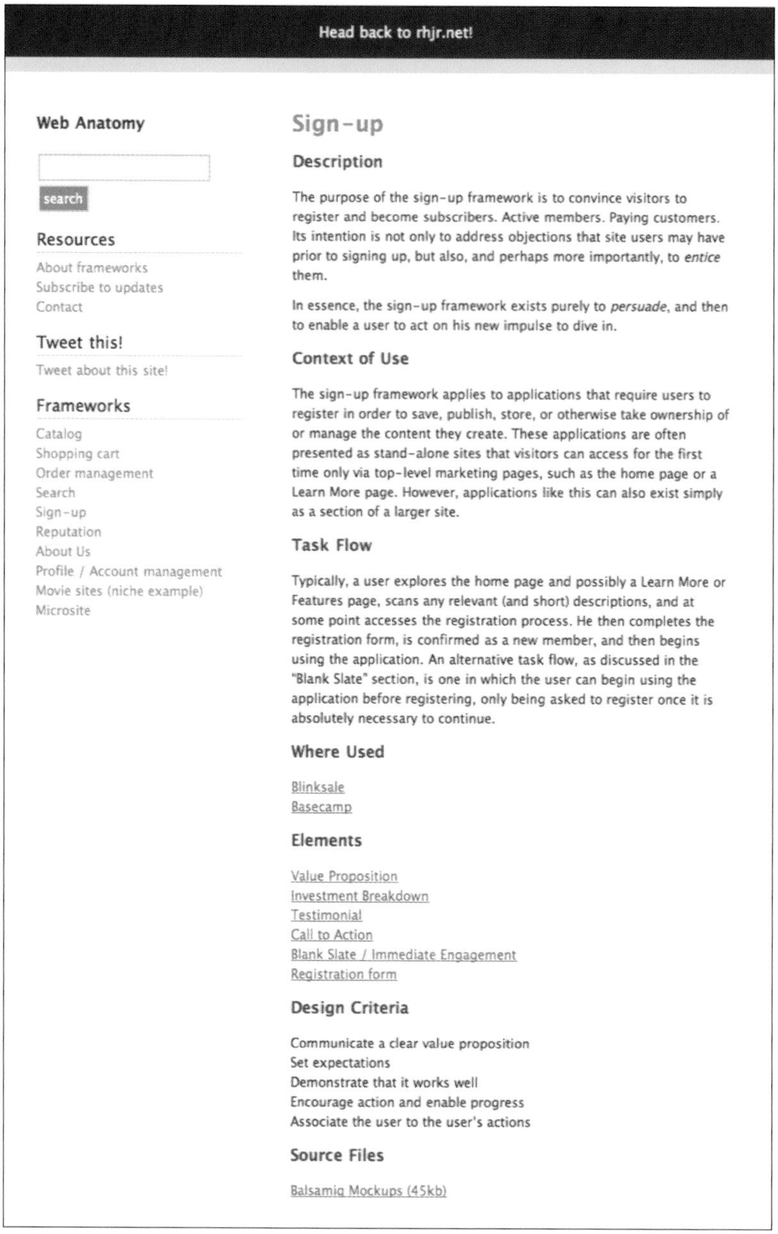

Web Anatomy

Resources

About frameworks
Subscribe to updates
Contact

Tweet this!

Tweet about this site!

Frameworks

Catalog
Shopping cart
Order management
Search
Sign-up
Reputation
About Us
Profile / Account management
Movie sites (niche example)
Microsite

Sign-up

Description

The purpose of the sign-up framework is to convince visitors to register and become subscribers. Active members. Paying customers. Its intention is not only to address objections that site users may have prior to signing up, but also, and perhaps more importantly, to *entice* them.

In essence, the sign-up framework exists purely to *persuade*, and then to enable a user to act on his new impulse to dive in.

Context of Use

The sign-up framework applies to applications that require users to register in order to save, publish, store, or otherwise take ownership of or manage the content they create. These applications are often presented as stand-alone sites that visitors can access for the first time only via top-level marketing pages, such as the home page or a Learn More page. However, applications like this can also exist simply as a section of a larger site.

Task Flow

Typically, a user explores the home page and possibly a Learn More or Features page, scans any relevant (and short) descriptions, and at some point accesses the registration process. He then completes the registration form, is confirmed as a new member, and then begins using the application. An alternative task flow, as discussed in the "Blank Slate" section, is one in which the user can begin using the application before registering, only being asked to register once it is absolutely necessary to continue.

Where Used

Blinksale
Basecamp

Elements

Value Proposition
Investment Breakdown
Testimonial
Call to Action
Blank Slate / Immediate Engagement
Registration form

Design Criteria

Communicate a clear value proposition
Set expectations
Demonstrate that it works well
Encourage action and enable progress
Associate the user to the user's actions

Source Files

Balsamiq Mockups (45kb)

This does not mean, however, that we expect you to write an in-depth discourse for each of your frameworks. Rather, we recommend your framework documents be no more complicated than your pattern documents.

Stick to the following sections and you'll be just fine.

Description

The Description section addresses not just a description of the framework—its overarching purpose—but also the question of what human needs it meets. The catalog framework, for example, covered in the next chapter, describes that people handle item-selection in a three-step process, and that this fact is the reason the catalog framework exists, as it directly supports that behavior.

We've done our best to include this type of information in each framework's Description section, but we're also sure you'll come up with different variations on the section as you develop your own framework libraries. The important thing to get across is what the framework is meant to handle. The catalog framework supports the process of item-selection. The search framework supports the content-finding process when site navigation doesn't cut it. The sign-up framework persuades users to convert from visitor to customer.

Context of use

This section describes the problem a user is encountering or need a user is trying to fulfill when a given framework comes into play. For example, the sign-up framework addresses questions a user is likely to have when considering the merits of a walled-garden style web application which she can't use until after she signs up. It offers insight into the features and benefits of the application, the cost/effort of trying it out, information on how to get started, and so on.

Beyond this, this section also describes where the framework sits in a site's information architecture. The sign-up framework, for example, most often lives among the top level marketing pages.

Task flow

Many frameworks are comprised by a series of interactions commonly experienced in a set order. Some offer pathways to information so users can answer their own questions as soon as they come up. In these cases, there is a task flow the user must follow. The Task Flow section simply describes that task flow.

The exception to this comes from frameworks that describe niche site types, such as movie sites (see Chapter 7), or any other group of patterns that are consistently, at least in some combination, used together to create a complete solution. A typical movie site includes, among other things, a trailer video, cast and crew information, and a synopsis. Movie sites don't usually include tasks, per se (at least not in the sense that users visit them to perform some productive function), so the Task Flow section is unimportant to the movie-site framework and is therefore not included. But since these elements all work together to do the job a movie site needs to perform—the job of convincing a person to see a movie—they constitute a framework.

Co-requisites

The Co-requisites section simply lists other frameworks that are necessarily used in conjunction with the one being described. For example, an e-commerce framework would be comprised of elements specific to the sale of products or services on a site (for the purposes of this book, we've rolled these up into the catalog framework). To properly support the tasks in that process, however, the e-commerce framework would be used alongside the search framework, to offer a secondary path for locating items; a shopping-cart framework, to handle communication about a purchase; and a checkout framework, to handle purchases. These are all co-requisites for the e-commerce framework.

Related

Related frameworks are ones that may serve similar purposes or support similar user or business goals as the one being described. In addition to the search and shopping cart frameworks used, an e-commerce site typically includes an order-management system and a customer-account system as well. These systems can be documented as frameworks, then linked to from the Related section.

Elements

The Elements section is one of the two most important parts of a framework (the other being the Design Criteria section, which follows), because it provides a list of the design patterns that fall under its canopy. As you'll see throughout the next five chapters, the list of elements is the meat of a framework. This is where a framework library merges with a pattern library—the list links to documentation for the patterns in the framework. It's in this way that a framework library is like a wrapper for a pattern library (we talk about this more in "The First Framework Library," later in this chapter). Frameworks—unlike patterns—create context and provide guidelines for complete solutions, but again, they are largely composed of patterns.

There are no frameworks without patterns. The two work hand in hand.

Design criteria

The other most important element of a framework is the Design Criteria section, which is simply a list of guiding design principles for a framework. But while this may sound simple, it can be the most difficult part of a framework to define.

Design criteria make up a set of instructions, stated as a list of rules, that express the motivations behind a design by making crystal clear what it needs to accomplish for a site's users.

The sign-up framework (Chapter 5), for example, includes the following design criteria:

- Communicate a clear value proposition.
- Set expectations.
- Demonstrate that it works well.
- Encourage action and enable progress.
- Associate the user to the user's actions.

Each criterion operates as a *directive* for a design.

There are exactly two reasons to create this list, and they are incredibly important.

First, frameworks help you *reverse-engineer* human behavior, and this list of design criteria is the expression of that understanding. The very act of identifying a framework's design criteria helps to burn the value of the framework into your mind so that you always know what to focus on when implementing one in your own project. In design, even the most subtle and seemingly meaningless details can result in significant differences in the usability, conversion rate, enjoyability, and meaning of a product. Knowing what is important about a given design ensures you can make those modifications intelligently.

Second, the ability of a framework to shed light on this human behavior enables you to then devise new solutions that meet the same purposes, so that innovations based on them continue to meet real goals and solve real problems. Simply put, the Design Criteria section of a framework tells you what needs to be accomplished should you decide to take a completely unique approach to your design.

In each of the five frameworks documented in this book, we use the Design Criteria section to show examples of how this has been done— sites that meet the goals of a standard framework in different and unique ways. We hope this helps you understand not only how to think about and apply design criteria, but also imagine the new solutions made possible as a result.

This emphasis on design criteria, however, brings us to another important point, that extrapolating these criteria from a framework can appear tricky and somewhat like an unexplainable, magical process. We don't believe this is true.

The only real trick to determining the criteria for a design is to ask yourself what the framework does for you or a site's other users.

Figure 2.8
The value proposition element from GetBallpark.com

By asking what the sign-up framework accomplishes, for instance, start by looking at the elements in the framework. One element is the **value proposition**—featured on practically every site that requires users to register. The invoicing application Ballpark (www.getballpark.com), as shown in **Figure 2.8**, uses the statement, "The better way to send estimates + invoices." By asking what that statement accomplishes, it's easy to see that its goal is to communicate the value of the application. It tells users what the application does and why it should matter to them. In this case, an element in the framework and a design criterion feature the same words. The element is called the value proposition, and the design criterion is "Communicate a clear value proposition." In other words, the elements sometimes exist for no other reason than to satisfy one of the criteria for the design.

Another sign-up element, as we discuss in Chapter 5, is the registration form itself. A registration form enables the user to create an account. This much is obvious. But what is the design criterion to be extrapolated from this fact? To determine that, ask yourself why the user must register. Users must sign up so that the actions they take on the site can be tied to them somehow, enabling them to retrieve their data, customizations, and so on, the next time they sign in. One design criterion for the framework, then, becomes "Associate the user to the user's actions."

A trickier example might be the search framework, discussed in Chapter 4, because the elements in the framework don't necessarily make their purposes clear. To determine the criteria for an effective search system design, you have to understand why people search in the first place. A user searches when other site navigation somehow fails to guide her to her desired content. To compensate for this, search provides a secondary method for finding that content. But this secondary method will fail just as easily unless the content she seeks includes at least some of the same words the user expects will help her find it. So the design criterion then becomes "Associate content to user terminology." It would be impossible to see this without understanding why people search and what makes a search successful, but these are questions that have been well researched, and that you can usually answer yourself with a little thoughtful investigation. Ask what makes a search successful and you'll probably answer with something that can be rephrased into a design criterion.

Yes, some criteria certainly are more difficult to sniff out than others, but hopefully these explanations show you that the process involves little more than asking questions about the framework and turning the answers into directives.

In each of the following five chapters, the Design Criteria section will help illuminate how to do this when documenting your own frameworks.

In the meantime, let's look at the conceptual side of frameworks—the philosophical underpinnings that make frameworks *tick*.

Qualities of a framework

Renowned information architect Liz Danzico (Happy Cog Studios, Bobulate.com) once gave a talk titled "The Framework Age." The presentation centered on the idea that instead of designing to support strict, scripted user behaviors, web designers have begun to design flexible platforms for user behavior. While Liz's talk focused on a shifting web paradigm that is unrelated to our topic, along the way she labeled three qualities of frameworks that, together, form a definition.

To reveal these qualities, Liz talked about the difference between classical music and modal jazz.

In classical music, she explained, every note is inscribed. A composer painstakingly writes out each and every note of each and every section of a composition for each and every instrument. To become a master player, one must bring finesse and grace and style to the table, for sure, but at the very core, one must bring the ability and discipline to *play the notes*. Perfectly. Every time. In classical music, to play an incorrect note is to fail.

Jazz, however, is very different. And modal jazz is almost the polar opposite.

Before recording the groundbreaking album *Kind of Blue*, legendary trumpet player Miles Davis walked into the studio and handed out six pieces of paper. These pieces of paper offered just a few bits of useful information— the key of a song, its tempo, and a few other constraints that would keep the musicians moving in the same direction. They offered nothing else.

Instead of playing compositions note for note, rigidly following the rules of a laboriously inscribed stack of sheet music, Miles Davis asked these musicians to compose in real time. To write the music as they played it.

He wanted them to perform. To improvise. To bring themselves out into the music.

Despite the fact that no one in the room had ever played in quite this way before, the next step in their evolution as musicians, and indeed the next step in the evolution of jazz, was laid out before them on six little pieces of paper.

And through this simple but revolutionary request, the world was introduced to modal jazz, which is essentially *music born of frameworks*.

While the shell of each song—its outline, its structure—was written down, everything else was left wide open. Musicians were free to play off of the framework however they chose. To experiment. To stretch their musical legs.

Through this analogy, Liz illuminated the three defining qualities of a framework.

Present

First, frameworks are **present**. In Liz's own words, they're "detectable, but not inscribed," which is to say they exist and can be identified, but their manifestations are by no means set in stone. Much as frameworks can be found in every musical genre, they can be found in site designs in virtually every vertical market. This makes them incredibly easy to sniff out and document, but they remain unique in as many ways as there are manifestations. Five billion different search systems may feature an essentially identical pagination interface, but somehow, in some way, every last one of them will differ from all the others. *Detectable, but not inscribed.*

Additive

Second, frameworks are **additive**. They enable designers to build upon and scale designs in whatever way makes sense for a particular solution, as well as string together collections of frameworks to compose entire sites.

Performance enabling

Finally, frameworks are **performance enablers**. They enable designers to stylize their designs. Customize. *Perform.*

Rather than confining users to some rote set of rules, frameworks allow for *improvisation*. Although the elements of a framework may remain largely the same in a majority of cases, each and every implementation of a framework must, like a design pattern, be adapted to work in its environment. A search-results page, for example, may be so common that it has become a standard part of every search system, but each one must be considered and designed in the context of the larger application. This is where the designer's aesthetic comes in. Here, the designer gets to inject style, nuance, finesse. Here, the designer gets to *perform*.

Informing innovation

So, while frameworks can simply serve as the starting point for a design, it's important to understand that, as standards, they do *not* represent the death of innovation. In addition to essentially giving us a set of snap-together interface solutions, frameworks offer insight into how to kick things up a notch or three.

Consider the major online retailers. You may have noticed they all use an extremely similar information architecture. On Target.com, for example, if you enter through the home page, you look around for links related to the products you want (for example, sports equipment), identify categories that may offer the items you're attempting to find, scan search results full of products, spot an item you want know more about, and then click through to the details page for a better look. (Granted, the high art of Googling has all but eliminated the need to follow this process while shopping online, but that's a different story.) Every major retail site on the web supports this core task flow.

Why?

Because the online version of the shopping experience matches our long-established mental model of shopping—in fact, it's practically *identical* to how we shop in real life. There's nothing magical about it. Target.com, Barnesandnoble.com, Amazon.com, and many other retailers online simply support typical human behavior.

The reason this matters is that someone had to notice the behavior, decide to support it online, and then design something that offered a representation of the offline behavior that rang true for users. These retailers decided to emulate real-world shopping behavior almost note for note, but they didn't have to. Once they understood the real-world human behavior, they could have invented wildly different solutions that solved the problem in a much more exciting way.

And therein lies *your* opportunity.

The very psychology that led to the design of every standardized solution out there can also lead to much more compelling designs. Put this psychology at the center of your decision-making process and you give yourself the ability to design incredible things that *still work well for users*.

Simply put, the point of a framework is not to limit innovation, but to *inform* innovation.

The first framework library

Frameworks, at the time of this writing, are in their infancy, illustrated by the fact that the book you now hold in your hands is the first to discuss them in terms of user experience rather than code. As such, we don't yet know of any *public* framework libraries. (Those we've curated before have been private.)

So we started one. It's at http://webanatomy.rhjr.net.

The Web Anatomy framework library includes documentation for all of the frameworks in this book and more. Our hope is to continue growing it based on *your* feedback, ideas, and contributions.

As you can see from the site, a framework library should be little more than a *wrapper* for a pattern library. This is especially easy, of course, if you've already created a pattern library for your organization, but even if you haven't, you can begin both by creating the framework documents using a wiki or another solution and linking the elements listed in the Elements section to the pattern documents that describe them.

In the Web Anatomy library, we've linked elements whenever possible to public pattern libraries. When the elements we listed were not available in public libraries, we attempted to describe them well enough to stand alone. We hope these elements will eventually be documented in other pattern libraries so we can link to them then.

Figure 2.10
The first public
framework library, at
http://webanatomy.
rhjr.net

Figure 2.10
The first public framework library, at http://webanatomy.rhjr.net

As the first public framework library, we've made sure it reflects the practices we recommend in this book. Used in conjunction with the book, the library will help you see not only how to document frameworks, but also how to share them. On its own, we believe the library will help anyone who uses it reap the very benefits we have detailed in this and the preceding chapter.

We also certainly hope it won't be the last public framework library, and that other individuals and organizations will open their libraries up to anyone who wishes to make use of them.

Rolling your own

As you can see, our library appears to be comprised of static web pages rather than presented via an openly editable wiki. In truth, the Web Anatomy library is built atop the popular content-management system and blogging tool WordPress, and it features a custom WordPress theme.

You can use any tool you like to create your own library. It's important, however, that the library be available to any and all of an organization's staff who can benefit from it, and that it be documented using a method that is efficient to update. (Trust us. For what we hope are obvious reasons, you don't want to document your framework library in *print*.)

Frameworks in the Wild

One interesting question that came up after Robert gave a workshop about frameworks at Jared's UIE Web App Summit event was in regard to whether or not frameworks would homogenize interaction design enough to put some interaction designers out of jobs.

The answer, definitively, is *no*.

To the contrary, one of our goals with frameworks is to enable designers to spend less time repeating tedious interface design and architecture tasks, and more time doing what these designers *should* be doing: focusing on user-experience vision and strategy for their organizations and clients.

Another workshop attendee asked how to prevent stringing these frameworks together in such a way that you end up with the interface equivalent of Frankenstein's monster. Our answer:

Frameworks, just like the human anatomical systems we are relating them to, fit together remarkably well. There is so much overlap and such strong relationships between them that their divisions easily become invisible, resulting in completely seamless interactions. In many cases, a single pattern can be part of multiple frameworks at once, and play multiple roles for a user. One example of this is a button labeled Register Now that is used both as a call-to-action to entice users to sign up for a conference and also as the entry point to the account-management con-version system the event organizers will use to correspond with the regis-trant before the event.

No individual framework has much meaning by itself. Even Google's search framework, clearly the dominant framework in play in the com-pany's core task flow, is accompanied by elements designed to orient users to the site, entice them to use more of Google's services, and sign in to retrieve previously stored information. It's only when woven together that frameworks constitute a complete site or application—a complete experience.

On to the frameworks

The following four chapters cover significant frameworks—catalog, search, sign-up, and About Us—in great detail. In these chapters we dis-cuss the human behaviors that made these frameworks standard, the results from research and usability studies that relate to them, and what types of things you should consider when putting the framework to use in your own projects.

In Chapter 7, we show you a framework for a niche market—the movie industry. We don't do this because we believe all our readers are involved in the movie industry (although you certainly may be), but rather to illus-trate how to identify the elements that make up a less common framework. Practically every industry has its own set of standards—higher-education sites have application forms, stock photography sites have admin tools for photographers, financial sites have portfolio-management tools—and we use this chapter to illustrate not only how to spot these industry-specific cases, but also how they work together with other frameworks to form complete sites.

When you're done, again, be sure to check out http://webanatomy.rhjr. net to see a living, breathing framework library as an aid to begin docu-menting your own frameworks and curating your own library.

On to the frameworks!

PART TWO

Frameworks

PRODUCT GALLERY

USER ID

PASSWORD

SIGN IN

CONTENT

NEWS

NEWS

Catalog

O dds are, the last time you walked into an unfamiliar grocery store, you took a look around to determine where the things you needed might be located. Ranch dip? That's probably on the snack aisle next to the potato chips. Steaks? Probably in the back at the butcher's counter. Asparagus? Produce section.

While spotting your favorite brand of ranch dip, though, did you notice all the other products that caught your eye along the way? Sure, there were the things you expected—chips, cookies, crackers—but what about those neat-looking things on the end-cap? The fancy new chocolate-dipped graham crackers that come in animal shapes that your kid is bound to love?

Had you not been there in person, you may have never known about them. Had you not managed to determine which aisle the ranch dip was on, you may have given up and gone without. Had you not been able to see your favorite ranch dip alongside all the others, you may not have found out your second-favorite brand was on sale.

Grocery shopping is an everyday sort of activity that most adults rarely view with a critical eye, but what if you're a web designer working on a commerce site, or a photographer with a portfolio site, or a design director for the web team at a news organization? You can learn a few things from grocery shopping.

Namely, because the act of getting oriented in an unfamiliar place and locating items by scanning an environment and narrowing options is so ingrained in our lives, the behaviors a user exhibits on a commerce site and those she exhibits in a grocery store are virtually identical. But the analogy hardly ends there. The catalog model used by e-commerce sites is also used in quite a few other contexts—in fact, it's the basis for an enormous number of sites.

And the design of a catalog can make or break a user's experience.

Description

When we make a selection from a catalog, we generally follow the same three steps. First, we winnow down our top-level choices. Next, we select one of the items from the collection. Finally, we validate our choice by looking over the item to make sure it's what we want.

But this process, which appears incredibly simple, is just as often supported online in devastatingly bad form as it is done well. You may not be familiar with the sites that have executed a solution to this process poorly, however, as most of them only exist on the Web for a short time.

Hopefully, you see our point.

To properly support the selection process, you must do far more than simply list out items and add price tags to them, but also far less than you might think.

Since our natural human behavior is to follow a three-step process in choosing an item, it's only logical that a supporting design address each step.

In direct conflict with the widely hypothesized notion that users hate to click, the catalog framework actually employs more steps than are needed from a technical standpoint, simply because human behavior demands it. (Incidentally, the notion that users hate to click is entirely false; users don't mind clicking at all as long as they believe their clicks are taking them closer to their target content.)

The elements in the catalog framework all work to support the selection process.

Context of use

Because so many activities involve item-selection, it can be surprising how many site types feature the same basic information architecture that we point to here as the catalog framework.

E-commerce sites support the activity of locating and purchasing products. *Library* sites support locating and checking out materials such as books, DVDs, and video games. *Portfolio* sites, for individuals and companies alike, support learning about and viewing examples of previous work. *News* sites support identifying and reading news stories and columns. The list goes on. And a great many sites support these activities in an almost identical fashion. It's so common, in fact, it's almost shocking that there are still sites on the Web today that fail to emulate this basic organizational structure.

Sure, each of these vertical sites brings with it a set of niche-specific solutions, but at the core of each of these (and many more site types) is a simple architecture that guides a user from high-level divisions to detailed, low-level content.

Unlike many other frameworks, the catalog framework isn't typically nested within a larger context—the catalog usually *is* the context. That is, most of the time, the catalog represents the site's core. There may be many additional branches in the information architecture, such as whole sets of pages dedicated to company information or experiential micro-sites, but since the catalog supports the core activity for most of these sites— the activity of locating and choosing items, for whatever reason—it is usually by far the most prominent and common task flow found in these site types.

That said, catalogs can certainly be but a small piece of a much larger site, and they can even be positioned in an almost *ancillary* way. Such is the case for Discovery Channel's site, Shopping.discovery.com, as shown in **Figure 3.1**.

The Discovery Store, as it's called, isn't the main event by any means. It is accessed by clicking a small graphic in the upper-right corner of the main site at Discovery.com, which primarily offers descriptions of the channel's shows and schedules alongside news, games, and video clips. Users visiting the site are more likely to arrive seeking information than opportunities to buy, so the store is presented separately, almost as an afterthought.

Figure 3.1
The Discovery Store catalog is a sub-section of the larger Discovery site.

Task flow

The catalog framework represents a basic task flow: users simply move from a high-level category page to a gallery of content within that category, and then on to a content page via the simple act of selecting an item to be viewed.

You've probably traversed this task flow hundreds, if not thousands, of times and perhaps not even realized it.

Co-requisites

Because many web users rely heavily on search functions to quickly locate items within a catalog, the search framework (see Chapter 4) is an essential part of any catalog site. As discussed later in this chapter, however, it's important that the roles of these two frameworks not be confused—they serve distinct purposes and should be viewed and treated as separate task flows.

Related

Many e-commerce catalogs enable and encourage users to create accounts so they can better manage items, orders, and so on, and increase their commitment to and investment in a particular site. For more about this, please visit webanatomy.rhjr.net, and learn about the account-management framework.

Elements

The catalog framework is composed of just four elements, but as you'll see, each one is incredibly important. They are the Category page, Gallery page, Content page, and Guided Links.

This rather unassuming list is the backbone for a huge chunk of the web as we know it.

Category page

First in the series of screens that compose the catalog framework is the *category* page. Jared's research team at UIE calls these "department pages" because they represent what's sold in a store's departments, but the term can just as easily be applied to a section of a news site, such as World News and Politics; a genre division in a music site such as Rock and Pop; and so on. In fact, a site's *home page* can often be classified as a category page with its high-level overview of site content.

To uncover the power of this type of page, UIE once took a hard look at the many different strategies for organizing content on sites.

In 2002, the team at UIE examined the e-commerce sites for a number of popular retailers to see how they handled the problem of categorizing large numbers of products, to see if the design teams behind these sites came up with different methods, and to see which methods were most effective. (The results of this analysis are discussed later in the chapter). Starting with a study on apparel and home goods, UIE looked at thirteen different sites, each with a similar product set.

Every site had similar characteristics. First, they split their content into just a few top-level categories, such as Women, Men, and For the Home. Second, they all offered *galleries* (more on this in the next section). And finally, their galleries all linked off to content pages (more on that in the Content Page section, below). **Figure 3.2** and **Figure 3.3** show a sample of a category list and gallery page.

Not much has changed since UIE's 2002 study—major e-commerce sites all still have category, gallery, and content pages in common. And category pages are what facilitate the first of the three item-selection steps: winnowing.

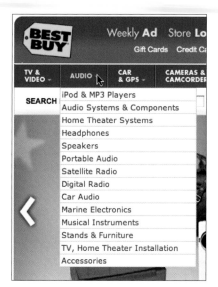

Figure 3.2
BestBuy.com features a
number of categories.

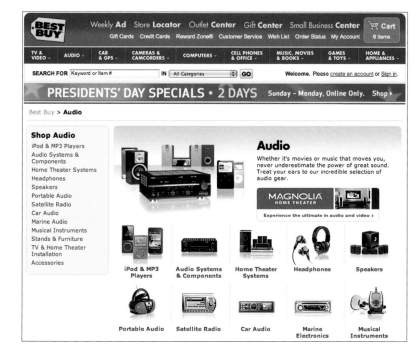

Figure 3.3
Like most online
retailers, Best Buy uses
gallery pages.

The pages do this by dividing the vast array of a site's content into high-level groups of related content that support a user's mental model of how those things relate to each other. The term Rock on a music-purchasing site should, and likely will, include any and all music that a user would consider rock music. The term Technology on a news site should link only to stories on technology.

NYTimes.com offers a number of major categories, including World, U.S., Business, Technology, and so on. Each category page does essentially the same thing as a department page on a commerce site: it offers a way to winnow down options and select a specific item. However, news sites often use a combination of category and gallery pages (discussed in the next section) in which the category page also offers links directly to articles instead of to gallery pages.

A subtype of the category page is what UIE calls the "search-department" page, which is a search results page that has been customized for certain search terms to offer department-style information. On BestBuy.com, for example, a search for iPod leads to a search-results page that looks more like Apple's home page than Best Buy's typical search results.

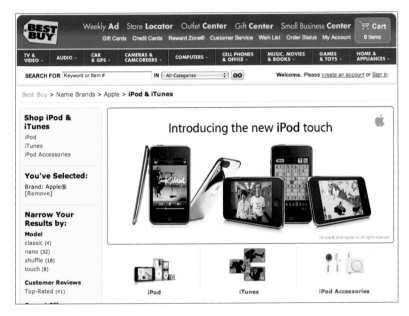

Figure 3.5
BestBuy.com offers search department pages for select products.

This approach might be taken for popular search terms, products that span several categories or break down into several subcategories, or perhaps because of promotional agreements with the product's parent company.

Search department pages don't usually live forever, though—they are often in place only for a short time, eventually replaced by standard search results once the search term no longer requires such extra attention. (For more about search department pages, see Chapter 4, Search.)

As you can see, grouping related content under major categorical headings simply helps a user weed out sections of a site that are irrelevant to her target content and hone in on the ones that are likely to meet her current needs.

From here, she can move on to selecting an item.

Gallery page

The *selecting* step—step two in the three-step selection process—occurs by way of gallery pages.

Galleries are a catalog site's hardest working pages. They are what separate those users who find the content they are seeking from those who don't. A well-designed gallery page will drive users to success every time, while a poorly-designed site will only serve to drive users away.

And in UIE's study, while the number of items and the specific information that was presented in each gallery varied, all of the sites basically presented the same types of information, such as the item's name and price (on commerce sites), as shown in **Figure 3.6**.

For a gallery page to be effective, it must answer any questions in the user's mind related to making a selection.

Figure 3.6
Gap.com offers product names and prices on its gallery pages.

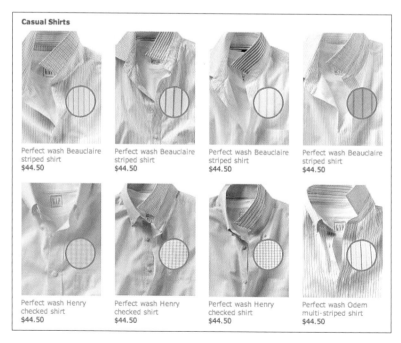

Suppose, for example, that Sony Ericsson wants you to purchase one of their mobile phones, and it has 17 models from which to choose. And suppose that to help you, the company provides a list of available phones on its web site.

W502a, C905a, C702a, C510a, W760a, X1, W595a, C902, TM506, W350a, Z555i, W380a, Z750a, K850i, W580i, P1i, S500i

Would you like the C702a or the X1? How about the TM506?

What's the difference, you ask? Sony Ericsson won't tell you until *after* you've chosen the phone you want. Only then will the site inform you about your chosen model's features.

What do you mean you can't decide? We've given you all the information that the designers of SonyEricsson.com give every user who comes to its site to view these phones. To discover which phone they want to buy, users get to choose from the preceding list.

Now, to be fair, the site does offer accompanying *images* of the phones.

Figure 3.7
SonyEricsson.com offers photos of its phones, but no descriptions.

Now you know which phone to choose, right? The X1 looks pretty slick. It probably has all the features you want. Right?

The designers at Sony Ericsson worked hard to create a gallery of all the available phones so users could choose one. However, they left out a critical component: the information that those users will need to make their choice. Unless the users are already intimately familiar with the phone they want, supplying model names and pictures doesn't help.

And Sony Ericsson's designers aren't the only ones who struggle with providing a gallery that can help users choose their desired mobile phone. The designers at Motorola did practically the same thing with their gallery page, as you can see in **Figure 3.8**.

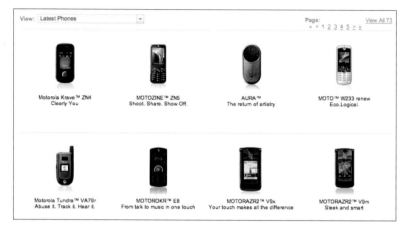

Figure 3.8
Motorola took the same approach as Sony Ericsson.

Besides the addition of pithy descriptions, Motorola's list doesn't give any more information for choosing a phone than the Sony Ericsson site. It's unlikely a user will pick the phone of her dreams from this list.

The design patterns used to facilitate item selection from a gallery page can vary wildly, and which ones get used depend entirely on the purpose of a site and the user's context and goals at any given moment. Following is a breakdown of some of the patterns that might be used within the Catalog framework to facilitate the selection process.

Quick Look

On commerce sites, the Quick Look pattern enables users to see a larger version of a product image without clicking through to the item's content page (discussed in the next section). Quick Look often also enables users to add an item to the shopping cart, choose basic configuration options (for example, color and size on clothing sites), and get fulfillment information, such as the item's price and estimated delivery time.

Item Identifier

Almost all gallery pages provide some sort of identifier for the items shown. A book on Amazon.com is identified by its name. An article on NYTimes.com is identified by its headline. A car is identified by its make and model.

Item Image

Item images simply provide a glimpse of the product to help the user discern its appearance from other items on a gallery page. Images are commonly used on commerce sites to show off products, and are usually offered as thumbnail-sized images—just large enough to entice the user to click through to the content page for an item.

Short Item Description

Short item descriptions provide high-level textual information about an item when item images are insufficient. For example, on commerce sites, a short item description is used when images of a product don't help a user discern the differences between products. When shopping for hats, images of each hat are useful, but when shopping for digital SLRs, which generally look similar to each other, images will be less helpful, so a short item description can help the user identify differences between items.

When a gallery lacks the information a user needs to make an informed decision, she has to resort to **pogo-sticking**. Named after the children's bouncing toy, the term describes those times when a user jumps up and down through the hierarchy of the site, hoping she'll eventually hit the content she desires.

When a user is locating accessories for phones she already owns, for example, she knows the phone model and she knows she wants to see which accessories are available for that model. In such a case, it's likely the Motorola gallery will work. But when the user is choosing a new phone—the next one she will purchase—she may not know the phone model, and the little information she may know about what she is looking for (for example, large, easy-to-press buttons or an email capability) isn't communicated in the gallery. She'll have to resort to pogo-sticking to complete the task, bouncing back and forth between product pages.

UIE's analysis of usability tests shows that pogo-sticking rarely helps users find their target content. In studies of e-commerce sites, for example, sixty-six percent of all purchases occurred without any pogo-sticking at all—the users purchased the first selection they chose from the gallery two-thirds of the time. And when users did pogo-stick, the more they did so, the less they purchased.

This extended to other catalog sites as well: studies showed that users who didn't pogo-stick found their target content fifty-five percent of the time, whereas those who did pogo-stick succeeded only eleven percent of the time.

To make this case further, consider the very complex process of buying a home. Applying for a mortgage, especially if you've never done it before, can be a confusing world of unfamiliar jargon.

Many banking sites handle mortgages similarly to Citibank.com, whose gallery page includes a section called What You Get. It states, without fanfare, that fixed-rate, adjustable-rate, and FHA/VA mortgages are available and it offers links to each one.

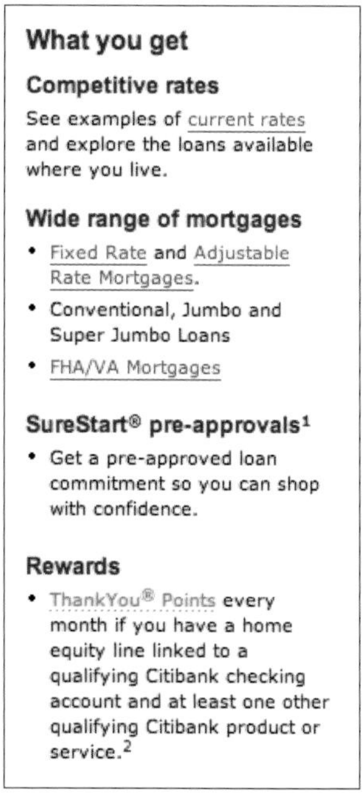

Figure 3.9
Citibank's gallery could work well if you already know what you need.

What you get

Competitive rates
See examples of current rates and explore the loans available where you live.

Wide range of mortgages
- Fixed Rate and Adjustable Rate Mortgages.
- Conventional, Jumbo and Super Jumbo Loans
- FHA/VA Mortgages

SureStart® pre-approvals[1]
- Get a pre-approved loan commitment so you can shop with confidence.

Rewards
- ThankYou® Points every month if you have a home equity line linked to a qualifying Citibank checking account and at least one other qualifying Citibank product or service.[2]

That probably works well if you already know exactly what you need, but what about home buyers facing these terms for the first time? How do they decide? It seems Citibank's designers assumed users would pogo-stick through the two choices to figure it out.

Clearly, it's important to include as much information on the gallery page as is necessary to inform a user's decision. For Sony Ericsson and Motorola, this could mean providing a short list of features next to the photo of each phone. For Citibank, it could mean briefly describing each type of mortgage, or dividing the page into subgroups, such as First-Time Buyers and Current Owners, to help the user better determine which mortgage is appropriate. On a news site, it could mean writing informative headlines that offer a glimpse into the story's content or displaying a snippet of the story itself.

Another bank, Wells Fargo, took a slightly different approach to its gallery of mortgage options. While it offers the same content, its galleries (and there are multiple versions, depending on which path you take through the site) provided copy to help users decide which link to click (for example, "Gives all qualified buyers the opportunity of putting only 3% down on a primary residence and taking advantage of flexible qualifying guidelines.")

It doesn't end there, however—the order of the items on the gallery page is also relevant. According to UIE's research, users expected the most important items to always be listed first in the gallery. In fact, they often didn't even realize when a list was sorted alphabetically—if the first few items weren't of interest, they often assumed the rest would be even less interesting.

Regardless of its effectiveness, it is from the gallery page that a user makes her selection and moves on to the content itself.

Content page

The content page, also called the details page (as in, Product Details), is where a user can finally validate her choice. She can finally review the content she stepped through the site to find. She can add the book to the shopping cart. She can read the article. She can scan the reviews and decide whether or not to purchase the digital camera.

In other words, the content page delivers the prize at the end of the hunt. On commerce sites, it may feature user reviews, information on relevant promotions,   usage and maintenance data, configuration options, and much more. On a news site, in addition to the desired article, it may offer sharing options, an RSS feed for the item's parent category, and perhaps even reader comments.

On Gap.com, as shown in **Figure 3.10,** the content page provides a short product description and information about how to care for the item, options to choose a size and color, and an option to view a larger image of the product.

Figure 3.10
Content pages on the Gap offers descriptions, images, and more.

On NYTimes.com, as shown in **Figure 3.11,** the content page offers a way to click through to the next article in the parent category, a link to the most popular articles for the category, and a commenting system so readers can discuss the story.

But content pages don't always deliver what a user needs to validate his or her decision.

Figure 3.11
NYTimes features links
to other articles and a
commenting system.

A common practice in the online consumer electronics industry, for instance, is to require retailers to hide a product's price from the shopper until she has put it into her shopping cart. Only after the shopper puts the product into the shopping cart is the price revealed. If the shopper then decides she doesn't want the product, she has to remove it from the cart to avoid purchasing it.

While watching people shop on sites that employ this practice, UIE's researchers have seen many shoppers show extreme frustration at the practice. When asked why they think the retailer does this, they feel it's some sort of trick—that the retailer hopes they'll make a mistake and buy an unwanted item by accident.

It isn't a trick, but rather a contractual requirement that the retailer has with the manufacturers. It's called the Minimum Available Pricing (MAP) policy and it allows large-volume retailers to sell products at a discount.

The agreement goes back decades, put into place to give smaller mom-and-pop retailers a competitive advantage against big box retailers. The original idea was that the big retailers couldn't advertise their lower prices (which are lower because of their huge ordering capability), but could share the price once the customer was in the store. When these retailers went online, the shopping cart had to emulate the in-store experience.

The retailers are trying to follow the rules and give their customers great prices, but the customers think there's something devious about it.

The designers at BestBuy.com came up with a clever workaround. They still require that the user take special action to see the price—as necessitated by the agreement—however, instead of showing the shopper a shopping cart with the product in it, they display a pop-up that has the price and two buttons: Checking Price—Remove from Cart and I Want To Buy—Keep in Cart.

Behind the scenes, BestBuy.com puts the product into the shopper's cart for the duration of the pop-up. If the user indicates she is just checking the price, the system automatically removes it from the cart. Only if she indicates she wants to buy the item does it remain in the cart.

When UIE's researchers measured brand engagement before BestBuy.com implemented this solution, they found a large dip in shoppers' perceptions of the brand after encountering a MAP situation. After making this change, UIE saw the brand strengthen. By investing in the new design, shoppers now feel BestBuy.com is on their side and is not trying to deceive them. Clearly, it's very important that the right information is conveyed to users as they try to validate selection decisions.

Once again, a variety of design patterns can be used to facilitate this task and influence the user's behavior. When it comes to a user's need to validate her item selection, in fact, the list of patterns is quite long. Following is a summary of many of these patterns.

Long Item Description

Building on the short description from the gallery page, the long item description simply provides an extended overview of the product, potentially including things like technical information for electronics equipment, editorial reviews for books, and so on.

Image Gallery / View Larger Images

In commerce sites, image galleries (usually containing just a few images) are often offered so the user can see the product in several ways, either in different contexts (clothing worn on different body types, for example) or at different angles (front, back, and so on). This type of gallery generally offers a View Larger option so that thumbnail images can be shown by default, thereby conserving screen real estate, while still providing a way for users to see larger versions of each image.

Fulfillment Details

This information lets users know how much an item costs and how quickly it can be delivered.

Availability

Item availability, in addition to simply providing status information, is often shown on a Content page to instill a sense of scarcity. A user who thinks a product has limited availability may believe the item is more valuable and therefore feel more compelled to order it.

An example from outside the world of goods and services is event sites. A professional conference may have a maximum capacity of 200 people. As seats are purchased, that number continually decreases, potentially making the remaining available seats more enticing to interested visitors who remain undecided.

Lists

On commerce sites, wish list and simple shopping list features can be provided to give users a way to mark items for future reference. This pattern can build commitment on the part of the user—the act of compiling a list increases the likelihood that the user will return to the site.

Configurator / Configuration Options

A pattern more complicated than most, the Configurator enables users to select from a series of customization options for a product. On a clothing site, the user may choose a size and color. When ordering a drum set, the user can choose the type of cymbals, drums, stands, and sticks she wants. On MiniUSA.com, a user can fully configure a Mini Cooper, save the result, and use it to order the Cooper of her dreams. By giving the user various ways to choose the exact configuration she wants, this pattern helps her feel comfortable that she indeed made the right product choice.

Social Influence patterns

Social influence patterns include *review*, *rating*, *recommendation*, and *referral* features—patterns used to influence a user by way of social behavior. Reviews are frequently offered on product pages to quell a user's concerns about a product. Ratings offer a fast mental shortcut for deciding whether or not the product is of reasonable enough quality.

Recommendation functionality gives users a way to put their stamp of approval on a product without getting so involved as to write a review. And a referral function enables users to tell their friends and colleagues about a product.

Again, the patterns used within the catalog framework can vary greatly depending on the purpose of a site and a user's goals at a particular moment, and it's vital that these patterns be chosen carefully.

Regardless, the Content page represents the end of the trail—the point at which the user finally makes a decision about whether or not to purchase an item, read an article, or something else. The user starts with an array of choices, she makes a selection, and she gets the information she wants.

Category. Gallery. Content.

Winnow. Select. Validate. Simple as that.

Guided links

In another study conducted in 2001, UIE looked at how to get users to find valuable content that they weren't already aware of upon first visiting a site.

This is an important problem when dealing with large sites in particular, because these sites are constantly adding content. E-commerce sites add new products. Product-support sites add hints for successful use. Intranets add new information to help employees be more efficient. How does a user discover the new content?

UIE's research showed that users were three times more likely to find this additional content if they used the category links on the home page instead of by using the site's search function. In an effort to understand more about why this was happening, UIE's researchers dug a little deeper into the data.

It turns out that one main clue is what people do *after* they find their target content.

Target content is the information that people come to a site to find. Studies show that most site visitors have a purpose on a site. For example, few people go to www.ups.com just to see what UPS is all about. Instead, they go when they have a specific need, such as tracking a package, finding the nearest drop-off location, or opening a new account. Users come to the site with a goal and do their best to achieve that goal. But what happens after they've achieved it? How do designers drive users toward that valuable content they didn't know was there?

UIE's research turned up some surprising statistics. Apparently, the way users get to the target content affects whether they'll continue looking or not.

UIE's study of thirty users found that if the participants used the site's search function to locate their target content on the site, only twenty percent continued looking at other content after they found the target content. But if the users used the category links to find their target, sixty-two percent continued browsing the site. Users who started with the category links ended up looking at almost *ten times* as many non-target content pages as those who started with the Search box.

Search, even when designed well, only lets users see what they are looking for. If they ask for shoes, they get shoes. But category links mimic what happens in real life. In a study that involved watching people shop in the mall (with their permission—not by stalking!), shoppers who went into stores specifically to buy shoes ended up purchasing other products, like sweaters, as well.

When users are exposed to the categories, they unknowingly become educated on the other content available on the site. Many users in the study told UIE's researchers that they were making mental notes to "go back and see" the other content while they located their target content.

With Search, there is no opportunity to see what else the site has to offer (unless Search is broken and therefore provides content the user didn't ask to see). Quite simply, Search is too specific.

Guided links are the solution to that problem.

Guided links are nothing complicated—they're simply links to other content within a site—but their existence is key to a user's ability to winnow, and as such, just about every category, gallery, and content page in every major catalog site on the web offers guided links.

On JCPenney.com, after you drill down into the Tees and Pullovers sub-category, (within the Shirts category in the Men's department), links are offered in the sidebar to gallery pages for many of the shirts JC Penney's offers.

Bestbuy.com's In-Ear Headphones sub-category offers links to galleries that highlight specific brands, features, price ranges, and even colors.

In the library world, Plymouth State University (http://library.plymouth.edu/) uses Scriblio, an open-source library catalog system built on top of WordPress, as the front-end of its catalog system. PSU's site not only offers the standard combination of category, gallery, and content pages, it also features guided links along the way so that a user can identify additional material relevant to target content.

Using guided links, users can access other titles by a specific item's author, galleries for related subjects, and even the library's full item record.

Guided links do exactly what they say they do: they *guide* users to other content. More clicks. More viewed items. More value for users. More goals met for the business.

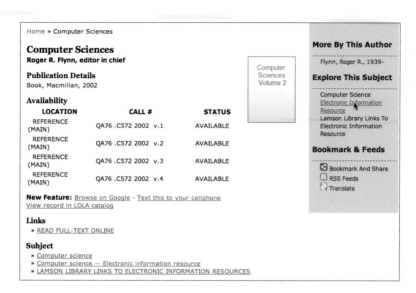

Figure 3.13
The Scriblio system for library sites features guided links.

Design Criteria

Back in UIE's 2002 study—the lessons of which are very applicable to this day, and which other, more recent research supports—the main difference between the sites studied were the category pages. Among the thirteen sites studied, UIE's researchers found five different types of category-page design. Most sites listed the categories in a left-hand navigation panel, with the galleries for that category listed in the page's main content area. However, some got clever.

The Gap and Victoria's Secret (www.gap.com, www.victoriassecret.com) both used menus rather than pages to present top-level categories.

Old Navy (www.oldnavy.com) used a combination department and gallery page on which the navigation sometimes contained galleries and sometimes contained products.

Lands' End (www.landsend.com) used a design containing both product descriptions and departments.

Finally, Eddie Bauer (www.eddiebauer.com) combined text lists of all the products in the department with a toggle to see the pictures for a gallery.

After realizing that there were five basic types of department pages, the goal became to see if the different types made a difference in user behavior. While UIE expected differences between individual sites, it wasn't clear if one type of design would outperform the others.

As with many of the company's e-commerce studies, UIE invited participants to its facilities with a list of products to buy. Participants were given the money to make purchases and told to purchase as many of the items on their list as possible. In this particular study, forty-four users shopped for a total of 687 products. After watching people shop on the sites, the UIE team compared their behaviors.

The sites with the standard left-hand navigation, such as Macy's, performed the worst, selling the least amount of product. Lands' End's design, featuring both product descriptions and department pages, performed the best. Old Navy's combination department-and-gallery design came in second.

In the study, the number of pages that a user visited before they put something into their cart was inversely proportional to purchasing. The more pages they visited, the less they bought. (Remember, these users knew exactly what product to locate and were ready to make a purchase.)

Looking at the number of pages visited before a user put something into the cart, users who traveled through Lands' End's design made purchases by visiting one-third as many pages as Macy's users. Lands' End users saw fewer visits to *wrong* galleries—galleries not containing the user's desired content (often forcing the user to hit the Back button—a clear sign of a problem).

These days, however, many sites with multiple levels of organization, such as BestBuy.com, support a user's winnowing process via several category levels spread across multiple pages, and it's a safe bet that major retailers wouldn't do this unless it worked in their financial favor. This tells us, then, that it isn't a high number of clicks that decreases a user's desire to buy, but rather a high number of *incorrect* clicks. The more pages a user visits that fail to deliver her target content, the less likely it is that she'll complete her task through a given site.

So the right path to innovation seems to lie in making the item-selection process more *accurate*.

To determine how to make the process more accurate, we must look at what the current standards tell us about human behavior and extrapolate design criteria that will lead to a new and improved design.

First, we know that people like to explore catalogs. It's the web equivalent of window shopping. A user who doesn't immediately know what she wants to purchase needs a way to look around and discover content. A user who knows what she wants but doesn't know what it's called needs a way to follow the scent of trigger words along the hierarchy to narrow down the possibilities. A user who knows exactly what she wants and even knows precisely how to search for it still needs the opportunity to look around and discover related items she perhaps didn't know existed.

Second, we know that users tend to follow the three-step item-selection process of winnowing, selecting, and validating.

Third, we know that even with a sound offering of guided links, not every user classifies content according to the same taxonomies through which most catalog sites are organized. One man's Trash is another man's Treasure.

How can we address these things?

How can we prevent *incorrect clicks* differently than through the nebulous goal of designing better category and gallery pages? How can we enable and encourage site exploration without knowing exactly which words every user associates with certain items? And is it possible to support the three-step item-selection process without strictly using the aforementioned catalog elements?

The answers are in the design criteria.

Support exploration

As previously mentioned, web users rely heavily on search functions to locate known items within a catalog. With this in mind, it can be easy to believe that a catalog site need not include all the standard elements, but instead rely exclusively on a site-wide search function. After all, search can deliver users to their target content much more quickly than by drilling down through an elaborate hierarchy of categories and content.

But as you probably realize, the fact that people use search functions doesn't necessarily mean they rely on *site-specific* search. In reality, they very commonly rely on outside search engines such as Google and Yahoo! to locate products and other items, and simply visit the sites that appear within the first few results. For this reason, and several others we'll discuss in a moment, it's vitally important not only that catalogs enable browsing methods, but also that the pages included in that process maintain unique URLs, as well as appropriate page titles and content. This way, search engines can index the content and these pages can appear in search results, thereby driving traffic to a site.

To put this in context, consider what happens when sites are not structured in this way by looking at the anti-pattern of the standard catalog architecture. (Whereas a design pattern is a common solution to a common problem, an **anti-pattern** is a common *ineffective* solution to that problem. It's a solution that should not be used, but is used frequently enough to have become a pattern and its ineffectiveness must be pointed out.)

The Clinton-Macomb Public Library site (http://cmpl.org) is built upon a library catalog system called Polaris. While it is purportedly one of the best library catalog systems on the market, Polaris goes against the standards established by the many successful sites that feature a catalog architecture, including the retailers discussed in this chapter. When users seek out content on the Clinton-Macomb library site, they are not given the option to browse through categories, nor are they shown gallery pages from which to choose items.

In fact, the system offers no category pages whatsoever, and item details are divulged entirely within search result pages rather than on separate content pages.

This is a problem for several reasons.

First, of the 687 shopping expeditions observed in UIE's e-commerce study, users only used the site's search engine twenty-two percent of the time. That means they used the categorization scheme to locate the desired products *seventy-eight percent* of the time. Since there are no category pages in the Polaris system, a user's basic and strongly preferred ability to *browse* is taken away. She has to search—there's no other way to locate content. The first step in the three-step selection process is *winnowing*. There is no winnowing without category pages.

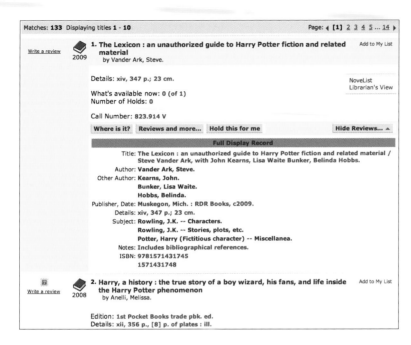

Figure 3.14
Polaris, problematically,
shows product
information within
search results pages.

As a result, serendipity is also stripped away—there's no way for her to *accidentally* discover the additional items she didn't already know about. She can only seek out the things she knows she wants, not those she *doesn't* know she wants.

Second, public libraries in particular depend on state and federal financial support for virtually everything—paying staff, holding library events, running community programs, funding collection development—you name it. Without the unique URLs that come from having content pages, catalog items cannot be separately indexed by search engines. The problem is obvious. Drive more traffic into the library and circulation goes up. Increased circulation compels the government to provide the library with more money, making it a better resource for its community, which in turn drives more traffic into the library. This all starts with a user's ability to find materials at her local library by running a quick Google search. By taking indexable content pages out of the equation, Polaris could be causing its customers to lose enormous opportunities.

Third, the lack of content pages (and lack of unique URLs for items within search results) hinders the user's ability to *bookmark content*. Without a unique URL, the user can, at best, bookmark the search results page, return to it later, and click to display item details within the results. (To Polaris' credit, users can indeed bookmark an item within the search results, but since the bookmark URL is created according to the item's current rank in the results and not its title or product ID, an item whose results rank changes in the future will result in a broken bookmark.)

Fourth, without separate content pages, the user is kept in the context of search results, attempting to validate her item selection through what is essentially a gallery page, where other items on the page can easily distract from the user's evaluation of the item. There is a quite a bit of information to be sorted through for any given product in a library cata-log, and showing it all within a set of search results makes for a muddled experience at best.

So why would Polaris design its catalog system this way? For the same reason many others do—to enhance its application based on a faulty understanding of a high-quality user experience. Often, web teams seem to think they can help their users simply by reducing the number of clicks it takes to accomplish a given task. This, of course, is patently wrong—the quantity of clicks doesn't matter one bit compared with the basic need for *clarity* as a user tries to complete tasks.

Incidentally, Gap.com currently employs a variation of this technique. Via a Quick Look option that displays when a user rolls over an item on a gallery page, Gap displays an overlay that enables the user to choose a size, add the item to the shopping cart, and other things (**Figure 3.15**). The key difference, we believe, is that Gap isn't using the technique to pro-vide *information* about the product—part of the winnowing process—but rather, they're enabling the user to *take action* on that item. And unlike Polaris, Gap uses this solution in addition to, rather than instead of, con-tent pages.

What this means is that it may be possible to consolidate the item-selec-tion process—not by stripping out the information and functions of the category, gallery, and content pages, but by distilling them down to one or two steps rather than three. This is risky business, of course—Polaris intended to do exactly what we've suggested and ended up with a search engine masquerading as a catalog that fails to meet the needs of either.

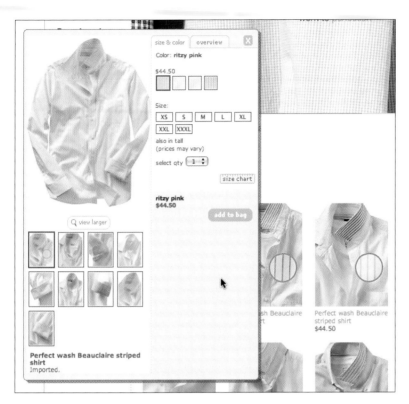

Figure 3.15
Gap.com offers a Quick
Look option, but still
provides a content
page.

But consider what Panic did when it started selling T-shirts online.

First, Panic offers a very limited selection, so the site doesn't need category pages.

Second, all of Panic's shirts are made the same way, so instead of listing product care information for each one, the company created a single About Our Shirts page. Shirts that come in different colors are shown side-by-side, instead of appearing on a single content page with a configurable color option. Clicking on a shirt produces a small popup window containing several more images of the shirt. The only other things a user needs to make a shirt selection are the ability to choose a size and quantity and add it to the shopping cart. Panic can meet this need *without content pages.*

Figure 3.16
Panic.com avoids using
category pages by
way of a single-screen
shopping interaction.

As seen in **Figure 3.16**, below each shirt image appears its price, as well as options to set an order quantity, choose a size, and add it to the cart. The shopping cart itself lives at the bottom of the page; users can either drag T-shirts into the cart or click the plus icon next to each shirt.

The sum total of all these factors is that Panic is able to deliver its entire catalog site through a single page, which not only supports a user's item-selection process, it also entirely avoids the problem of incorrect clicks. The user is never at risk of visiting an irrelevant page and having to click the Back button to retreat and begin again.

We don't have access to the results of any usability studies of Panic's site, nor have we seen its metrics, but the site has offered essentially the same design for several years running, so we imagine the approach is working well for the company. If nothing else, it offers catalog designers a fresh idea.

NYTimes offers another alternative with its experimental Article Skimmer, located at prototype.nytimes.com/gst/articleSkimmer/.

Using a wildly untraditional design, NYTimes offers a way for users to quickly scan the top stories for any given category simply by clicking category names and scanning headlines. Sure, NYTimes.com already supports this behavior, but the Article Skimmer does so in a very different way—it consolidates the headlines from all the top stories into a single

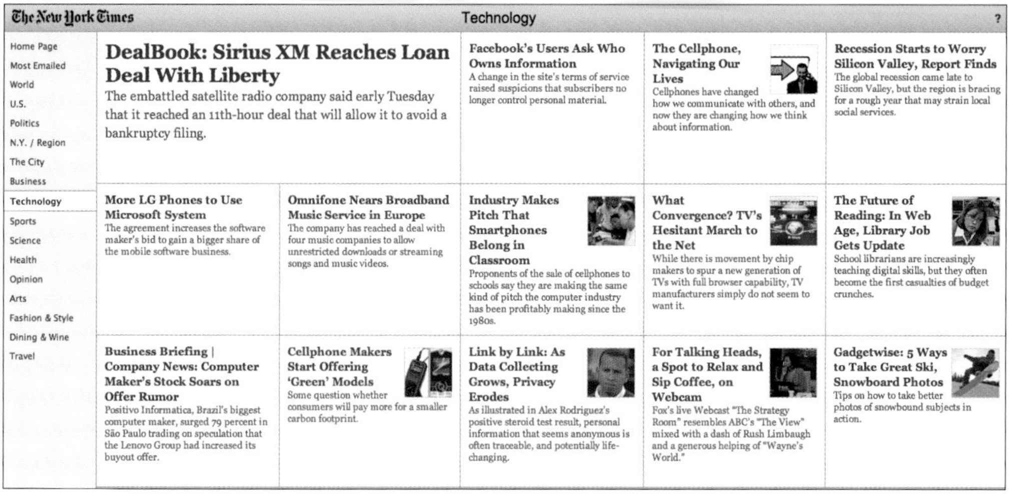
The New York Times | Technology | ?

Home Page
Most Emailed
World
U.S.
Politics
N.Y. / Region
The City
Business
Technology
Sports
Science
Health
Opinion
Arts
Fashion & Style
Dining & Wine
Travel

DealBook: Sirius XM Reaches Loan Deal With Liberty
The embattled satellite radio company said early Tuesday that it reached an 11th-hour deal that will allow it to avoid a bankruptcy filing.

Facebook's Users Ask Who Owns Information
A change in the site's terms of service raised suspicions that subscribers no longer control personal material.

The Cellphone, Navigating Our Lives
Cellphones have changed how we communicate with others, and now they are changing how we think about information.

Recession Starts to Worry Silicon Valley, Report Finds
The global recession came late to Silicon Valley, but the region is bracing for a rough year that may strain local social services.

More LG Phones to Use Microsoft System
The agreement increases the software maker's bid to gain a bigger share of the mobile software business.

Omnifone Nears Broadband Music Service in Europe
The company has reached a deal with four music companies to allow unrestricted downloads or streaming songs and music videos.

Industry Makes Pitch That Smartphones Belong in Classroom
Proponents of the sale of cellphones to schools say they are making the same kind of pitch the computer industry has been profitably making since the 1980s.

What Convergence? TV's Hesitant March to the Net
While there is movement by chip makers to spur a new generation of TVs with full browser capability, TV manufacturers simply do not seem to want it.

The Future of Reading: In Web Age, Library Job Gets Update
School librarians are increasingly teaching digital skills, but they often become the first casualties of budget crunches.

Business Briefing | Company News: Computer Maker's Stock Soars on Offer Rumor
Positivo Informatica, Brazil's biggest computer maker, surged 79 percent in São Paulo trading on speculation that the Lenovo Group had increased its buyout offer.

Cellphone Makers Start Offering 'Green' Models
Some question whether consumers will pay more for a smaller carbon footprint.

Link by Link: As Data Collecting Grows, Privacy Erodes
As illustrated in Alex Rodriguez's positive steroid test result, personal information that seems anonymous is often traceable, and potentially life-changing.

For Talking Heads, a Spot to Relax and Sip Coffee, on Webcam
Fox's live Webcast "The Strategy Room" resembles ABC's "The View" mixed with a dash of Rush Limbaugh and a generous helping of "Wayne's World."

Gadgetwise: 5 Ways to Take Great Ski, Snowboard Photos
Tips on how to take better photos of snowbound subjects in action.

Figure 3.17
The NYTimes article skimmer makes quick work of scanning headlines

viewable space. It even shows snippets from each article to better inform a user's decision to click or not to click. This makes it possible to scan the top stories from across the entire site in as little as a minute or two.

At the most basic level, we must support a user's need to explore a catalog without explicitly searching for known items or categories.

Beyond this, though, we can ensure that users find content according to their own mental models about what those items are called.

Expose the taxonomy

In order for users to find content according to their ideas about what the content is, what it means, and what it should be called, we can offer users the ability to create their own tags for content, thereby associating a variety of terms to each item to improve its findability.

Amazon faces a constant organizational nightmare—it offers millions of products, all of which users must be able to find on demand and by accident.

While Amazon led the way back in the early '90s by dividing its content into sections via a tabbed interface, it eventually outgrew the very same model it made famous. There were simply too many categories. *Too much content.* While the company has gone through many variations on its navigation scheme since then, one of the more intriguing options it has offered is the ability for users to tag products.

Figure 3.18
Amazon.com lets users choose their own words for organizing products.

Instead of clinging to a stringent taxonomy of its own making, Amazon handed the reigns over to its users and made the taxonomy extensible (thereby turning it into a **folksonomy**). Amazon customers can now decide for themselves how products should be classified. In the future, they'll be able to find content again according to their own preferences, and they may help countless other users in the process by creating tags that match other users' trigger words.

Encouraging exploration and expanding the possibilities for what terms site visitors can use to locate content are not revolutionary concepts by any means, but as design criteria, they can certainly lead to new ideas. With any luck, one day we'll see major commerce, library, knowledge base, news, and other catalog-based sites following a paradigm that supports user needs without transposing real-world processes into web interactions verbatim.

Maybe one day, a week's worth of grocery shopping will be done with just a couple of clicks.

Search

Google is arguably the most trusted name in the world when it comes to search tools. In fact, users are frequently put off when an on-site search engine doesn't look or work like Google, and as a result question whether it can be relied upon for high-quality results. Without knowing exactly what's so effective about the search master, most people simply trust it. For many, it's a fact of life—puppies are cute, bugs are icky, and Google just works.

But how did Google get to be so good, and how can we apply lessons from Google to on-site search to generate effective results and commonsense interactions? What elements do we need for a good search engine interface and how do they need to work?

At first glance, the search framework might appear simple. For example, in July 2008, Chiara Fox of Adaptive Path had this to say about one of the framework's key elements (http://www.adaptivepath.com/blog/2008/07/14/designing-search-checklist/):

> *Recently on projects I've found myself designing a number of search results pages. While each project has its own set of requirements and nuances, I think there are a handful of elements that should be included in most all result page interfaces. If you start out with this list, and then tweak as your situation requires, I think you'll end up with a pretty good page.*

Here are the items on my checklist, in no particular order:

- *Highlight the query term in the results.*
- *Restate the query on the results page.*
- *Show the number of results that were found.*
- *Include Previous and Next buttons, as well as links to additional pages, to move through results. These should be smartly linked; no link on Previous if you are on the first page and so on.*
- *Include a query box so the user can search again.*
- *Don't show the URLs of the result pages, unless your audience is... [tech-savvy] enough to derive meaning from the URL.*
- *Have meaningful page titles and descriptions for each result.*
- *The page title should be the link to the result.*
- *Allow sorting and refinement tools if appropriate for your users and content.*
- *Indicate if a result is not a regular page (e.g., a PDF file).*

Chiara's list is indeed a good start and should be no surprise. However, while the list of elements to include here is nothing shocking, there's far more to designing a good search framework than the results page alone, and there's far more to consider when adapting this framework to your own site than meets the eye. And that's what the bulk of this chapter is about.

The true challenges of search are in understanding why people search in the first place, how they use the results, what types of results to show, what information to include in them, and how to handle each possible type of search outcome. Once again, the elements of the framework themselves aren't meaningful until they're put into the context of the problems they solve.

Description

The search framework lets users locate specific content using a consolidated task flow as an alternative to traversing a site's hierarchy via its global and local navigation. By searching for items directly, users can frequently bypass the exploration process: instead of looking through category and gallery pages, users simply pull up a set of content links related to a specific query and click straight through to content pages. There's no need to negotiate the site's navigation and risk making a wrong choice.

Of course, only in a perfect world with a perfect user is search really that simple. In reality, search brings a whole set of problems of its own, each of which you will need to consider when adapting the search framework to your own designs. To understand these considerations, we must first understand the psychology that makes search necessary.

Context of Use

Web designers often say they spend a great deal of their limited time and resources working to improve their on-site search engines because, they believe, some people always rely on the search engine to reach their target content. They find further support for this assumption from Jakob Nielsen, who, in his book *Designing Web Usability* (New Riders), asserts that more than half of all users demonstrate "search-dominant" tendencies by going right to the search engine when they first visit a web site looking for content.

If this were true, designers would have their work cut out for them. Devising and producing a site that supports both visitors who prefer using the search engine and those who gravitate toward links presents a substantial challenge. Teams with limited resources find themselves having to support two separate paths to the same content. With perhaps thousands of pages of content, maintaining separate location tools becomes a monumental task.

In 2001, UIE's researchers put the user search-dominance theory to the test by conducting a study on e-commerce sites.

In the study, thirty users performed 121 different shopping tasks. Each user visited between three and six websites, shopping for items they were interested in purchasing. No two users were interested in exactly the same products.

If the search-dominance theory were true, a subset of these users should have always relied on the search engine to find product information, while others relied on the links. If at least a few users didn't consistently rely on the search engine, then the idea of search dominance would be in question.

Also, when looking individually at each site in the study, not all the users who visited a particular site should have employed a single strategy; samples of each kind of user behavior should have come up with each site.

To illustrate this point, consider the city or town where you live. Some of its inhabitants are right-handed, some left. In any restaurant in town on a Saturday night, you should expect to find some mix of lefties and righties. It is highly improbable that only right-handers would populate a random restaurant on a random Saturday night. UIE had a similar hypothesis for these web sites: it seemed highly unlikely that only search-dominant users would use a site during a given series of tests. Some of those users were bound to use links more than search.

The data from the study showed that there wasn't a single user out of thirty who always used the search engine first when looking for product information. While users often suggest that they have a preference for search, none of the users in the study actually were search-dominant. There were, however, some *link-dominant* users. About twenty percent of the study participants, in fact, chose links exclusively.

But even stranger, on fifty-three percent of the sites tested, each visitor stuck with a single location strategy—the same strategy employed by all the other visitors to that site. On twenty-one percent of the sites, *every single user* who visited the sites used search exclusively, and on thirty-two percent of the sites, users used only the links on the site. (The remaining forty-seven percent were a mixed bag, with users using both search and links.)

This implies there is something inherent to a site's design, rather than each user's hard-and-fast preference, that causes users to choose either the search engine or the links.

In other words, it appears that certain *sites* are search dominant, not users.

The data also indicated that one of the factors that predicted whether users would initially start with search or with links was the type of product being sold on the site. Certain types of products lend themselves better to being searched. For example, users typically rely on search to find a specific book or CD (more on this later), but tend to use links to find a particular item of clothing. The nature of the content on the site, it seems, can play a huge role in whether it is a search- or link-dominant site.

Users also often gravitated to the search engine when the links on the page failed to satisfy them in some way. Users seemed to use the search engine as a fallback after failing to pick up **scent** (a sense of the correct path to take to locate information) on the home page. UIE's study produced more evidence to support this behavior. UIE's researchers observed many home-page link failures that forced users to rely on the search engine.

Put another way: remember the winnowing step of item-selection that we identified in the catalog framework? Well, search is what gets used either when users can't sufficiently winnow on their own via catalog navigation or when the items being sought are easily searched for by name.

The lack of evidence to support the user search-dominance theory implies that teams may need to think about concentrating their efforts on a single content-location method. Depending on the specific content on the site, teams might want to focus specifically on either the search engine or the links, not necessarily both. UIE's testing suggests that focusing the resources on a single approach can dramatically improve the user's experience.

Regardless, it's clear that search is primarily used not because some people strictly prefer it or because it's faster, necessarily, but rather because a site lacks the trigger words a user may be seeking, or because of some other design-related reason. **Trigger words** are words that match the user's mental model of what she is seeking—for example, a Lunch Specials link when a user is seeking information on lunch specials.

Plainly and simply: the number one reason people use search systems is to *resolve an error condition*—the error of being unable to find content via site navigation.

Task Flow

When all the planets in the solar system are properly aligned, the task flow for a search is simple: the user enters a search term into an input field, clicks an accompanying button, often labeled "Search," and is taken to a results page that lists possible matches to her query. The user clicks the first result, which, naturally, goes to the exact content she wants to find, and is taken to the content page for that item.

In the article "The Power of Defaults" (http://www.useit.com/alertbox/defaults.html), in fact, Jakob Nielsen describes a 2005 study performed at Cornell University in which users clicked the top item in a set of search results forty-two percent of the time, regardless of whether or not it was the best result. Eight percent chose the second result. Even after the researchers switched the top two results, users still chose the top result thirty-four percent of the time. In short, users *really* want to believe the search engine always offers the correct result first.

So what happens when it doesn't? Do users click the Back button, read through the rest of the results, and make a second, more appropriate choice, perhaps sifting through several pages of results to find the right one? Hardly.

Rather than go through ten pages of results—or even more than one page—a user is far more likely to modify her search term and run a new search. Only a small percentage of users will continue on to a second page of results, whereas most users, most of the time, will opt to modify the search term.

Clearly, this simple three-step task flow—*enter search term, view results, click*—is far less reliable than it may appear. We continue this discussion throughout the rest of this chapter.

Elements

The elements of the search framework are few but powerful, and they facilitate the search process from beginning to end for users who find themselves in need of alternative pathways to information when site navigation proves insufficient.

The search framework is comprised of the Quick Search, Search Results, Advanced Search, Filters, and Pagination design patterns. Unlike many patterns, however, these patterns can subdivide into multiple types depending on the purpose and scope of the solutions they address.

Quick Search

Quick Search is frequently nothing more than a simple input field with an adjacent button for submitting search queries, placed on the page where it can be found quickly and easily. But it's also frequently more compli-cated, and there are quite a few factors to consider when designing one.

Figure 4.1
Cancer.gov's Quick
Search implementation
is representative of the
most typical form of the
design pattern.

Most important is to understand why users jump to Quick Search in the first place: this insight should serve as the basis for all subsequent search-related design decisions. As we've already discussed, users don't rely on search simply because they are search-dominant people, but rather because some content lends itself to search very well, or because a site otherwise lacks a user's trigger words. To put this in context, consider the difference between sites such as Amazon.com and Cancer.gov.

Amazon has one of the best on-site search capabilities on the web. But surprisingly, the reason it works so well is the same reason that search may *not* work so well on your site.

Amazon's vast collection of books, CDs, DVDs, and videos make up what we call **uniquely-identified** content, which users easily search for simply by entering specific information—which they frequently already know. That is, people identify books by title and author, and they identify CDs by artist, title, and song titles. Almost every time a shopper looks for a specific book or a CD on Amazon, she types in one of these identifiers.

For instance, when a book shopper in UIE's study entered *Sum of All Fears*, Amazon returned seven different editions of the Tom Clancy book. Amazon didn't suggest any other books containing the words *sum* or *fear* in the title—just seven editions of that single book.

When users search for uniquely-identified content and the users know what those identifiers are, then search works very precisely. In a UIE study conducted with thirty-five online shoppers, the search returned useful results ninety-nine percent of the time for CDs and videos.

But this process of searching for uniquely-identified content is the excep-tion to the rule. In most cases, users are looking for content for which they don't already know the name. Consider the behaviors most likely put in practice on these four sites:

- Amazon.com contains mostly uniquely-identified content, and users are very likely to know (and therefore search by) a product's name, or some reasonable facsimile.

- BestBuy.com contains mostly uniquely-identified content, but because electronic equipment often features meaningless model numbers, users are less likely to know or search for these products by their exact names (like *Mitsubishi WD-65735*) and therefore more likely to search by category or product type (such as *hi-def television*).

- Gap.com contains some uniquely-identified content, but since clothing items frequently have nonspecific names, users are very likely to search by category or product type, with occasional exceptions.

- Cancer.gov contains mostly non–uniquely identified content, and since it's unlikely users know the names of articles on the site, users are very likely to search by topic rather than by the name of a piece of content.

On Amazon, you can search for a Harry Potter book by its title, its author, or a variety of other identifiers, but this is only true because Harry Potter–related items *have* identifiers. In UIE's study, however, for non–uniquely-identified content such as toys, apparel, or pet supplies, search only worked thirty-one percent of the time. Most web content lacks these memorable identifiers, making it very difficult to produce a decent set of search results. And indeed, this is where Amazon starts to get into trouble. In addition to selling books, the site offers electronics (among a huge variety of other types of products). What terms did users in UIE's study enter when searching for a DVD player? Well, they didn't enter *Panasonic DVD-RV31K DVD Player (Black)* (the product's actual name). They didn't even enter *Panasonic* (the manufacturer). When users sought DVD players, they typed *DVD player*.

This is typical for non–uniquely-identified content. When looking for a pair of Frye boots, one user typed *boots*. Another user, looking for colored pencils, entered *craft supplies*. A user looking for pearl earrings typed not *earrings*, just the very generic *jewelry*.

While there are non–e-commerce sites that have uniquely-identified content, they are rare. The United States Patent and Trademark Office (PTO), for example, lets users look up trademarks by attributes such as name, trademark holder, and the attorney of record. Search for *James Spool* under the attorney of record, for example, and you'll get a peek into Jared's father's work. But the PTO is the exception, not the rule. It is more likely that the majority of content on your site will fall into the non–uniquely-identified category.

And even on sites full of uniquely-identified content, there are exceptions when users want to find something by a means other than using the identifiers. For example, one user who had been listening to Celtic music every morning on the radio wanted to purchase a good introductory CD to the genre. Typing *celtic* into Amazon's Search box revealed 889 results, but provided no sense as to which CD would be a good introduction.

In other words, although designers are often incredibly tempted to follow Amazon's lead, the site you should probably pay the most attention to from the list above is the one that matches the model of most sites: Cancer.gov.

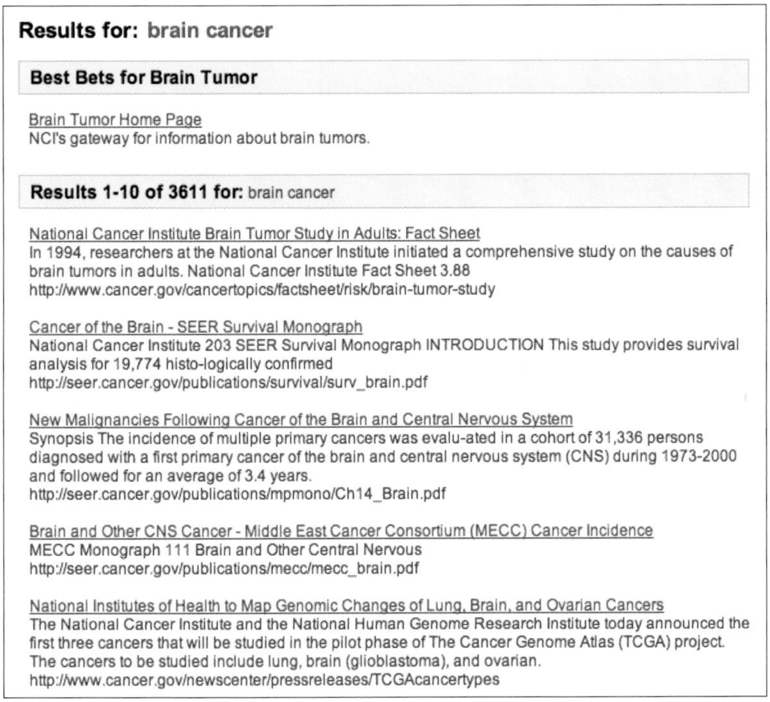

Results for: brain cancer

Best Bets for Brain Tumor

Brain Tumor Home Page
NCI's gateway for information about brain tumors.

Results 1-10 of 3611 for: brain cancer

National Cancer Institute Brain Tumor Study in Adults: Fact Sheet
In 1994, researchers at the National Cancer Institute initiated a comprehensive study on the causes of brain tumors in adults. National Cancer Institute Fact Sheet 3.88
http://www.cancer.gov/cancertopics/factsheet/risk/brain-tumor-study

Cancer of the Brain - SEER Survival Monograph
National Cancer Institute 203 SEER Survival Monograph INTRODUCTION This study provides survival analysis for 19,774 histo-logically confirmed
http://seer.cancer.gov/publications/survival/surv_brain.pdf

New Malignancies Following Cancer of the Brain and Central Nervous System
Synopsis The incidence of multiple primary cancers was evalu-ated in a cohort of 31,336 persons diagnosed with a first primary cancer of the brain and central nervous system (CNS) during 1973-2000 and followed for an average of 3.4 years.
http://seer.cancer.gov/publications/mpmono/Ch14_Brain.pdf

Brain and Other CNS Cancer - Middle East Cancer Consortium (MECC) Cancer Incidence
MECC Monograph 111 Brain and Other Central Nervous
http://seer.cancer.gov/publications/mecc/mecc_brain.pdf

National Institutes of Health to Map Genomic Changes of Lung, Brain, and Ovarian Cancers
The National Cancer Institute and the National Human Genome Research Institute today announced the first three cancers that will be studied in the pilot phase of The Cancer Genome Atlas (TCGA) project. The cancers to be studied include lung, brain (glioblastoma), and ovarian.
http://www.cancer.gov/newscenter/pressreleases/TCGAcancertypes

Figure 4.2
Non-uniquely-identified content makes for more complicated search result requirements.

When trying to locate non–uniquely-identified content, site navigation (such as category links) is the way to go. On Cancer.gov, when searching for an article on, say, brain cancer, users will be more satisfied using the site navigation rather than by searching. A user is unlikely to know an article by its name or author when visiting the site for the first time (or even the tenth), and therefore will locate content one page at a time, one link at a time. And this isn't a bad thing; UIE's research indicates that, contrary to popular opinion, users don't mind clicking a few more times as long as they believe each click draws them closer to reaching their intended goal. And increasing the number of pages a user views creates opportunities for businesses to expose that user to more content, including ads.

The caveat, of course, is that this approach only works when a site provides the right trigger words. Users turn to search functionality when they can't spot their trigger words—when site navigation fails them. In other words, when people use search systems, they're trying to find links to content they couldn't find otherwise. They're trying to create links that *aren't already there.*

(For an in-depth look at trigger words and how they affect a user's ability to locate content, Jared's report "Designing for the Scent of Information" is available for purchase at http://www.uie.com/reports/scent_of_information.)

You can safely rely on your site's search system when you meet all three of the following conditions:

1. Your content is uniquely identified.

2. Your users are familiar with the identifiers.

3. Your users want to use those identifiers as the mechanism for locating the content.

To determine whether or not you meet these conditions, look no further than your search logs. If you spot a lot of category names, like *jewelry* or *men's pants*, instead of specific content references, then your content is non–uniquely identified content. If you don't meet any of these conditions, you'll need to find another navigation strategy for your users to succeed.

Beyond this strategic view of search, there are also quite a few low-level details to consider, such as a search field's position on a web page, its constancy throughout the site, field label, button label, and whether or not to offer a category menu or autosuggest functionality. We're leaving these details, however, to the curators of design pattern libraries. Our intention is not to document these patterns in this book, but rather to offer insight into why they are included in this framework and how they affect a user's experience with searching on a site.

Search Results

There are just two types of search results pages and four possible outcomes for any given search.

The first type of results page is the Search Gallery, and it's the one with which you are probably most familiar. It's simply a gallery, like that in the catalog framework discussed in Chapter 3. The only significant difference is that the collection of results presented on a search gallery page is created entirely on-the-fly based on the user's search.

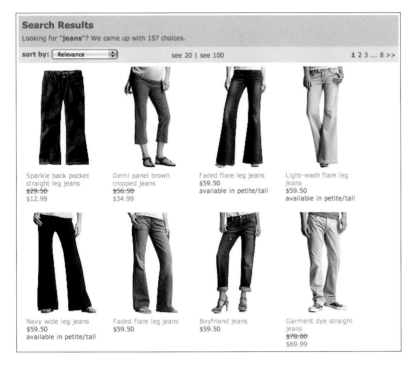

Figure 4.3
Gap.com features a search gallery, the first type of search result page.

In other words, the search gallery is a straight results page. The one you expect to see every time you run a search. The one Google uses.

One significant caveat with many search galleries is that they suffer the same problem as standard galleries: in the vast majority of cases, search results all receive the same treatment regardless of which design patterns might be most helpful for specific items. Since images are helpful for many items on Bestbuy.com, such as headphones, images are then used for *all* of Best Buy's products, including digital SLRs (single-lens reflex cameras), where images become significantly less helpful.

Regardless, search galleries are by far the most pervasive type of results page. In fact, every search engine we've ever seen delivers results in this format, including those that also offer the second type of results page: the **search department** page.

A search department page is a set of results that closely resembles a category page from the catalog framework. It may look different than the other category pages on a site, but its scope is the same. It presents links to an array of galleries and encourages users to further winnow their options before showing them a specific gallery. The search department page is basically a trick the designers use when a site has results that span too many categories to intelligently organize them in a search gallery page.

A shopper's search for *Nintendo Wii* on Bestbuy.com, for example, could be a daunting challenge for site designers. Does the user want the Wii game system, games that go with the system, accessories, branded clothing, toys, or something else? There's simply no effective way to guess the user's desires, and the only way to cull this truckload of possible items into a search gallery is to organize them into labeled sections. Of course, once you do that, you create, essentially, a category page.

Figure 4.4
BestBuy.com offers a search department page to highlight products related to the Nintendo Wii game system.

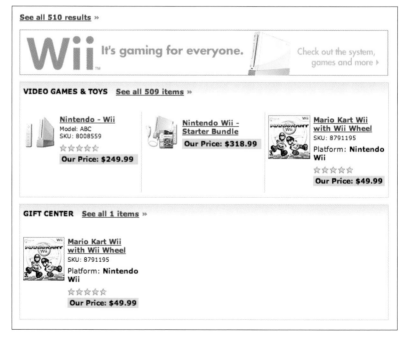

Search Outcomes

Regardless of the type of results page, there are four possible outcomes for a search.

- **Exact or very relevant match.** The user is offered results that lead her directly to the content she is seeking. This happens when the user searches with terms that match those used by the site and, specifically, within the content the user is seeking. This is ideal, as it puts the shortest distance between the user and the desired content.

- **Related items.** The results are related to, but not quite, what the user is seeking. This might occur when the site lacks the exact content the user is seeking or when the user searches using slightly different terms than those that would lead to exact matches.

- **Irrelevant results.** The user is offered results that are in no way related to the content she is seeking. This happens, of course, when a user searches using terms that don't match the site's terms, but it also happens when a search system is ineffective. For example, a search on *Men's Pyjamas* that returns every result that contains *Men* isn't helpful.

- **No results.** The search yields no results whatsoever. This occurs either when users search using too many keywords for the site to produce matches, when a user misspells search terms, or when the site simply has no matching, or even relevant, results. Particularly rigid search systems might also show no-results pages when the user simply uses natural language rather than specific tags. No results can be good if no relevant content exists on the site, but if the content is there and the user simply isn't finding it, it's a problem.

The first outcome in the above list is by far the best. The other three, however, can lead to disaster because, as it turns out, users really don't try too hard to succeed with search. In looking at the search patterns of thirty users shopping on e-commerce sites, UIE's researchers focused on those search attempts where search failed to help the user find a result. Interestingly, forty-seven percent of the users who failed only tried the search engine a single time. Another thirty percent tried twice. Less than twenty-five percent tried more than twice to get the search engine to produce a successful result.

Now, the designers of many of the tested sites went to great lengths to get users to continue searching. They put in encouraging search tips that said things like, "Try a new search using different terms." However, there was no evidence that these tips encouraged any user to search again. They mostly assumed that the first (or maybe second) try was the best they were going to get. For example, Bed Bath & Beyond's site encouraged a user who was searching for curtains to "use a generic term like *pans* or *coffee* to broaden [her] search and increase the number of items found." What, exactly, is a generic term for curtains? These results indicate that designers get one, possibly two chances to help users find their content via search. If most of the users don't find what they want in the first try, it is unlikely they will ever find it.

Incidentally, these results aren't unique to e-commerce sites. For years, similar results have been seen on intranets, corporate and institutional information sites, and any other type of site with a search capability. The data from UIE's e-commerce study simply proves what has long been suspected. More and more, UIE's ongoing research indicates that search has to be perfect. Users expect it to *just work* the first time. Every time. Most search systems, however, don't even come close. In fact, the more times the users in this study searched, the less likely they were to find what they wanted. On a single search, users found their content fifty-five percent of the time, whereas users who searched twice found their content only thirty-eight percent of the time. None of the users in the study who searched more than twice ever found their target content. The users (less than 25 percent) who persevered still did not reach a positive outcome.

The number one motivator for revising and running new searches was the "no results" message in response to a query. Most users give up when they see it (although some do try their query a second time).

Here's what happened in the study:

- On the first search attempt, twenty-three percent of users got a message indicating there were no results.

- Of the users who kept going, forty-four percent got a no-results message on the second attempt.

- If they still persisted, fifty percent got a no-results message on the third attempt.

- One-hundred percent of those who persevered through a fourth attempt got a no-results message.

In theory, as people use a search system, they should get better at making it perform. After all, each successive interaction is an opportunity to learn the idiosyncrasies of the tool. But in UIE's study, users didn't seize the opportunity. For users who didn't succeed up front, things went rapidly downhill.

Encouraging users to continue with helpful hints doesn't help. As we mentioned before, many sites provide hints on the "no results" pages that try to encourage users to enter different search terms. Unfortunately, the presence of these hints didn't improve the odds that a user would get better results the next time around.

A telling fact is that the users in the study were asked specifically to go to sites that had the content they were seeking, but one out of every five users landed on a no-results message on their first attempt. This indicates that there is something fundamentally wrong with the design of many search systems.

The key for designers seems to lie in getting users relevant results on the first try. The sites that do are most likely to succeed.

Advanced Search

The most known version of advanced search is likely the one accessed via an Advanced Search link, usually positioned next to a Quick Search field. But this is probably not the most frequently used version. How can this be so?

To begin with, advanced search in its traditional form isn't as widely used as one might expect. Informal observation has shown us that it's extremely rare to come across a group that consistently uses advanced search, and outside that group, it's hardly used at all. In fact, it's possible that the only people who really *care* about advanced search are librarians, and perhaps people in similar situations. Librarians have an almost constant need to find very specific information for customers, and this information is often obscure enough that a plain old search just won't cut it. These searches may involve not only finding obscure information, but also locating the information in specific media types or in certain editions or versions, and being able to verify the reliability of the information. Advanced search can work wonders for cases like these. But most people aren't in this situation most of the time. For most users, most of the time, advanced search is overkill.

But there is a second type of advanced search that is used quite frequently, and it doesn't at all appear advanced. We'll call it Qualified Quick Search.

Qualified Quick Search is a form of Quick Search that requires additional criteria—qualifiers beyond keywords—to be effective. The search requirements on travel sites are a prime example.

For example, to book a flight on Southwest.com, users are asked to choose the departure city, arrival city, departure date, return date, and the number of adults and children who need tickets. The car rental site Hertz.com asks for the city where the car is to be rented, pick-up and drop-off times, and the desired car type. To book a hotel room on Hilton.com, users specify the city and state in which they'll be staying, check-in date, check-out date, how many guest rooms are needed, and whether or not to expand the search to all Hilton hotels and to a wider geographical area.

Figure 4.5
Hilton asks users for check-in and check-out dates as part of its Qualified Quick Search.

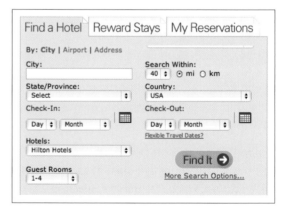

For any of these sites to provide good results, they need to know a lot more information than that the user wishes to "schedule a trip to Atlanta." They can't deliver meaningful results until they have an exact collection of details.

> ▶ **Clinical Trials**
>
> **Search for Clinical Trials**
> What Is a Clinical Trial?
> Clinical Trial Results
> Educational Materials
> List a Trial in NCI's PDQ®
>
> ▶ **Cancer Topics**
>
> What Is Cancer?
> Treatment
> Prevention, Genetics, Causes
> Screening and Testing
> Coping with Cancer
> Smoking
> Cancer Health Disparities
> NCI Fact Sheets
> Physician Data Query (PDQ®)

Figure 4.6
Cancer.gov points users to a separate search option specifically designed for clinical trial searches.

Cancer.gov offers a variation of this, also with the goal of meeting a specific need. Users looking for clinical trials are unlikely to know how to search for them through the site, so the site designers created a page enabling users to search for clinical trials, which includes a variety of qualifiers. What makes this different than advanced search? Frankly, nothing, save for the choice in wording. Instead of an Advanced Search link, it offers a Search for Clinical Trials link. The problem with advanced search is that users don't necessarily think they have advanced problems, but rather simpler problems they don't know how to solve. Simply changing the label can change the user's level of agreement with the functionality.

Supplying the search form for clinical trials also educates users on the factors distinguishing one trial from another. A trial's status, phase, treatment type, ID, and sponsor are all things that narrow down the options. But if their only option for doing so were a Quick Search field, would every single user on the site know to enter all of this information? Not a chance. But they may learn from this alternative functionality and apply that knowledge later on.

Amazon and many other sites offer a simpler case. Since typical search terms can fall across a number of categories (such as the search for the Nintendo Wii, whose results span electronics, toys, clothing, and others), these sites often add a drop-down menu to their Quick Search implementations. In doing this, they ask users to qualify their search terms with specific criteria, much in the same way that Southwest asks users to qualify their search with departure and return dates.

This, then, is a version of advanced search, in that it requires qualifiers beyond that of simple keywords. But it's also quite different from advanced search, because these criteria are usually required rather than optional, and few criteria are needed, whereas advanced search frequently offers a vast array of filtering options. It's simpler—it asks only that a user better qualify her search before running it. Hence, Qualified Quick Search.

When designing an on-site search system, it's important to consider whether or not advanced search is necessary. There may be a selection of users who will occasionally benefit from it, but if your site is like most— that is, its primary users are not librarians—you can probably get away with not building an advanced search page. If, however, you need very specific information from every user before you can deliver any sort of meaningful results, Qualified Quick Search may be the perfect solution.

Filters

Filters are another form of advanced search, with two key distinctions.

First, filtering options usually appear only after an initial search has been run, with the goal of helping users reduce the options generated by an initial search, while at the same time increasing the accuracy of the results. On the travel-booking site Kayak.com, as shown in **Figure 4.7** for example, once a user has specified her initial qualified search criteria, such as her travel dates and destination, Kayak's search results page offers a sidebar filled with options to further narrow down the choices. This elaborate set of filtering options would be overwhelming if presented on the home page, where the goal is to get the user started as painlessly as possible, but on the results page—in the *context* of search results, alongside them—this sidebar gives the user the power to see how she might further improve her results, and do so without modifying her search to include all the information the site needs to generate better results.

Second, filters can be presented in a wide variety of ways. They can be as simple as keyword links that go to subcategories or other content pages; or they can be as elaborate as a collection of sliders, check boxes, and radio buttons that trigger real-time updates. Kayak offers these real-time updates as well. By limiting the airlines and times of day a user prefers to fly, she can easily pare down the results to see only those that perfectly match her criteria. And this happens as soon as the user changes a setting in the sidebar filters: the list of search results auto-updates so she can almost immediately see the effects of the changes rather than wait for the page to reload with a new set of results.

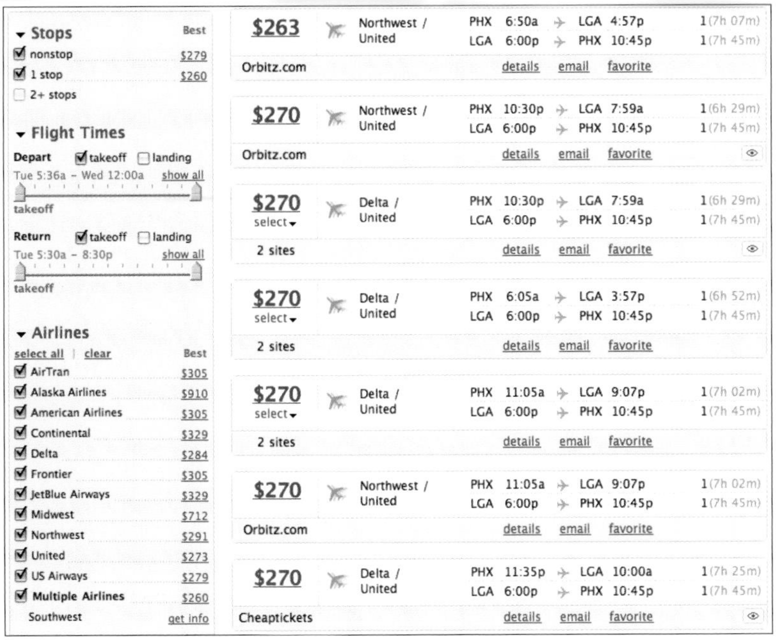

Stops	Best
☑ nonstop	$279
☑ 1 stop	$260
☐ 2+ stops	

▾ Flight Times

Depart ☑ takeoff ☐ landing
Tue 5:36a – Wed 12:00a show all
takeoff

Return ☑ takeoff ☐ landing
Tue 5:30a – 8:30p show all
takeoff

▾ Airlines

select all | clear   Best

☑ AirTran	$305
☑ Alaska Airlines	$910
☑ American Airlines	$305
☑ Continental	$329
☑ Delta	$284
☑ Frontier	$305
☑ JetBlue Airways	$329
☑ Midwest	$712
☑ Northwest	$291
☑ United	$273
☑ US Airways	$279
☑ Multiple Airlines	$260
Southwest	get info

$263 Northwest / United PHX 6:50a → LGA 4:57p 1(7h 07m) / LGA 6:00p → PHX 10:45p 1(7h 45m)
Orbitz.com details email favorite

$270 Northwest / United PHX 10:30p → LGA 7:59a 1(6h 29m) / LGA 6:00p → PHX 10:45p 1(7h 45m)
Orbitz.com details email favorite

$270 select▾ Delta / United PHX 10:30p → LGA 7:59a 1(6h 29m) / LGA 6:00p → PHX 10:45p 1(7h 45m)
2 sites details email favorite

$270 select▾ Delta / United PHX 6:05a → LGA 3:57p 1(6h 52m) / LGA 6:00p → PHX 10:45p 1(7h 45m)
2 sites details email favorite

$270 select▾ Delta / United PHX 11:05a → LGA 9:07p 1(7h 02m) / LGA 6:00p → PHX 10:45p 1(7h 45m)
2 sites details email favorite

$270 Northwest / United PHX 11:05a → LGA 9:07p 1(7h 02m) / LGA 6:00p → PHX 10:45p 1(7h 45m)
Orbitz.com details email favorite

$270 Delta / United PHX 11:35p → LGA 10:00a 1(7h 25m) / LGA 6:00p → PHX 10:45p 1(7h 45m)
Cheaptickets details email favorite

Figure 4.7
Because they feature a background color used throughout the search results design and don't stand out, Kayak's filtering options can be difficult to spot.

The caveat to using filters is that for users to take advantage of them, they have to first *notice* them, and this can actually be trickier than it might appear. Kayak users often entirely ignore the sidebar full of filtering options and instead scroll through as many results as it takes for them to find the flights that match their needs. (Because travel-related searches almost always begin with a Qualified Quick Search, and because Qualified Quick Search typically asks for specific information without allowing the entry of free-form search terms, travel booking is one of the few situations in which users persevere through a potentially large number of results without modifying their search criteria.) Of course, going through all those results can be quite time-consuming, but users who don't notice the filters often appear to think that doing so is their only option. The key, then, is making sure the filters are noticeable. If positioned in a sidebar, for example, filters can be made more noticeable via the use of a background color that stands out against the background of the search results page itself. One site Robert reviewed recently used the same background color in the sidebar as in the page's header area (orange, when the results area had a white background), and as a result, the company's usability tests showed that users were not having much success finding and using the filters. (Your results may vary, of course, but as a rule, color contrast is a very good way to draw the eye to a specific page area.) But again, there are many ways to present filters—a sidebar full of filter controls is but one of them. The designers at Orbitz.com made its filters appear as part of the search results themselves.

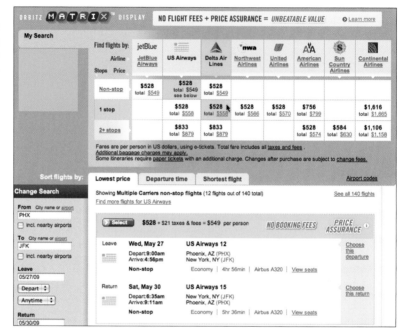

Figure 4.8
The Orbitz design team integrated filters into the result set.

Along the top of the results area, Orbitz features a matrix showing a selection of airlines offering flights at different price points. As the user hovers her mouse over a square in the matrix, an alternative background color is shown to highlight that square, as well as the column and row headings that indicate the number of stops on the trip and the airline offering the flight. Since the prices themselves are shown, the matrix blends right in with the results themselves, making the filters a seamless part of the search process.

Figure 4.9
Google puts its filtering options directly in context—in line with other results, at the bottom of the page.

As you can see in **Figure 4.9**, Google takes an arguably simpler approach: suggested search terms are offered via two rows of links at the bottom of each results page, allowing the users who make it to the bottom of the page to simply click once to run a modified search. That is, if the user actually sees the links. And as we've pointed out, the odds aren't particularly great that a user's results will improve beyond the first search.

Pagination

As part of its status as the gold standard in search, Google has popularized many design patterns, one of which is the pagination pattern. The interface, which offers a series of linked page numbers that are bookended by Previous and Next buttons, enables users to navigate back and forth between a set of search results pages, as well as skip ahead or back several pages at once.

Google may not have been the first site to make use of this particular pattern—it was used by several popular search engines prior to Google's inception back in 1997—but the all-powerful search site almost certainly made it the most popular version of a pagination interface on the web. Since Google implemented the pattern, it's been emulated on countless systems, including other major search sites, and even a huge number of catalog sites from news to commerce. Unlike most others, however, Google opted to instill a sense of playfulness into the design by increasing the number of letters (specifically, the letter *O*) in the name *Google* according to how many numbered page links are shown on a given results page.

Gooooooooogle ▶
1 2 3 4 5 6 7 8 9 10   **Next**

⊕ Add a result - See all my SearchWiki notes - See all notes for this SearchWiki - Learn more

Figure 4.10
Google's pagination interface, the defacto standard for search systems.

Although this playfulness contributes to the personality of the Google brand, it's by no means a necessary quality. The important part, from a usability perspective, is that the interface provides a method for getting back and forth within a series of pages. And it does that just perfectly. Showing page numbers sets an expectation that there are more results that can be easily accessed. Offering Previous and Next buttons with adjoining arrow icons gives users a sizable hit area and keeps them from struggling with the much smaller numbered links. Styling the current page number differently communicates to users where they are in the set of results pages.

It's when designers get crafty with pagination design, in fact, that things start to get messy for users. The prime example of this is the so-called infinite scroll pattern. The idea is simple: rather than distribute results across a series of pages, all results are loaded into a single page. On paper, this makes sense, as it eliminates the need for users to click to access results beyond the initial set and wait for new pages to load. However, infinite scrolling breaks a number of expectations for users and causes quite a bit of confusion (and perhaps even a broken keyboard or two).

Based on informal observations, because users expect to encounter the pagination interface at the bottom of results pages, the lack of one can be an unwelcome surprise. For example, in an informal study, users were asked to find a specific photograph buried deep within a set of results for an image search with an infinite scroll. One user, who was typical of the users in the study, went to great lengths to reach the end of the page. At first, he used the mouse to drag the scrollbar down. When this didn't work, he moved his mouse to the small arrow control at the bottom of the scrollbar and began clicking repeatedly to see if that helped. When this failed him, he resorted to the down-arrow button on the keyboard. When even this didn't help, he began pressing the button with more force, apparently believing that the sheer power of his intention would give him the desired result, much in the same way a video game player twists his body in all directions hoping to manipulate a character into moving in the right direction. Eventually, he started mashing down the button with enough force that the sound was audible in a screen recording of the experiment. That poor keyboard took quite a beating that day.

Again, puppies are cute, bugs are icky, and Google just works.

On a more thematic note, the pagination interface is a good example of the limitations of design pattern documentation. On the popular pattern library site Welie.com, the pagination pattern (which the site calls the "paging" pattern) includes a problem description that simply states, "Users need to browse through a large list of items looking for the item that interests them most." While this statement indeed describes, quite literally, the problem that the pattern solves, it doesn't say anything truly meaningful about the user's real problem. It doesn't reveal how the pattern fits into the larger context of searching—the when, how, and why of search. Here again is why frameworks are a necessary evolution of design patterns. Frameworks put design patterns back into context.

Design Criteria

In part, the design criteria for the search framework are a reaction to the category framework, because search is the fallback option for users when category navigation fails. As we've seen, for search to be effective, it must not only work immediately and according to users' expectations, it must also support the use cases where site navigation simply doesn't get users to the information they need.

Contrary to many frameworks, however, the design criteria for search are remarkably obvious. The rules are no different than what you should do for almost any site, for any audience.

Offer multiple paths to content

One way to improve search, counterintuitively, is to take the focus away from search by improving navigation throughout the rest of the site. Again, design criteria are the motivators behind a design—rules about what the design is intended to accomplish for users. It is for this reason that "offer multiple paths to content" is a criterion for the search framework. When a site's content predominantly comprises non–uniquely identified content, the best way for a user to accomplish her goal of finding information is to entirely avoid search and rely instead on pathways through the site's information architecture.

In practical terms, this means that the very thing that causes users to search in the first place can actually help improve the rest of your site. Remember, people search when the site's navigation has somehow failed them. By poring over users' search habits on your site, you can identify ways to tweak the navigation or information architecture to improve their ability to find the content without search. This is not to say you should rely exclusively on site metrics for all your decisions—on the contrary, you should put the site metrics in context by watching users to sort out why they search the way they do—but you can certainly make some changes based on metrics alone. If you can clearly see that lots of people are searching for *jeans* on your men's clothing site, it's likely they are not finding a link to the category in the expected place, alongside other category navigation. If the terms being searched are generic enough to qualify as categories, then primary navigation can be tweaked. If the terms are lower level, such as *baby-doll T-shirts*, then you can change the navigation within the Women's Ts category to make these items more findable.

However—and this should go without saying, but it's a typical enough reaction that it bears mentioning—don't make changes to your site navigation based on search terms that were entered just a few times. Look for clear and obvious trends. Usually, only the top search terms are candidates for changes to the navigation. When you base site changes on minor actions rather than major trends, you make task completion more difficult for the majority just to enable the edge-cases of the minority. Never sacrifice ease of use for the many based on the actions of the few.

Associate content to user terminology

When organizational words on the site don't match the user's trigger words, the user is more likely to search, to identify and try out an alternative method of locating content. However, it would be a nightmare for most sites to try to include every possible trigger word on every page; and in fact, doing so would likely dramatically decrease the site's usability. So when users do go to search, it's vital that it work exactly as expected. To this end, it's important to associate site content with as many different terms—keywords, tags, and so on—as possible so that any search term a user enters will lead to good results. This **metadata**—information about information, data that describes data—is vital to creating a search system that *just works* the first time. Every time.

Figure 4.11
Taking action increases a user's commitment to a site, so Amazon puts its users to work while simultaneously building user loyalty.

Suggested Tags from Similar Products (What's this?)
Be the first one to add a relevant tag (keyword that's strongly related to this product).

Check a corresponding box or enter your own tags in the field below.

- user experience (24)
- interaction design (23)
- ui design (23)
- interface design (21)

- usability (17)
- web design (17)
- design (13)
- ux (10)

- internet (4)
- information architecture (3)
- deliverables (2)

Your tags: [   ] [Add]
(Press the 'T' key twice to quickly access the "Tag this product" window.)

Help others find this product — tag it for Amazon search

Amazon puts this idea to work by encouraging users to associate products with keywords themselves (**Figure 4.11**). By allowing users to designate their own keywords for a given product, Amazon not only continually builds its library of associated keywords, it also gives users yet another way to become involved with the site.

Make the content easy to identify

Memorable things are findable things.

When searching for a digital camera, it can be quite difficult to remember a name that includes a model number like XJ7220. A camera named the Echo 3, on the other hand, is easier to remember, which then makes it easier to talk about with other people and search for on a site. When content is named using simple terms, it is easier for you to remember it, search for it, and communicate it to others.

You may not have any control over what products are named, but you might influence naming conventions for all sorts of other content on your site. You can create shorter article titles, for example, to make them more memorable. Page titles can be kept short and simple so that users can easily recall them later on. The page title "The Art and Science of Our User Experience Strategy Process" is much less memorable than "Our User Experience Strategy."

However, it's important to use the short and long versions of content links at the right times. In a site's main navigation, short and concise is better. "About Us" is a perfectly appropriate label for global navigation, as it says what the subsequent page is called and what it is likely to contain (information about the organization). Within content, however, and search results pages, it's generally better to use longer link labels, as they help a user feel confident that the subsequent page will indeed contain the content she expects. For example, the statement "We've done several experiments in this area" (with *experiments* as a link) leaves a sense of ambiguity. Where will the link on experiments lead? Will it be another site? A page listing this organization's experiments? A page that describes just one of the experiments? The revised statement "We've done several experiments in this area, including one in which we tested a cat's ability to defy gravity" is far more likely to leave the user feeling confident that the link leads to a page about an experiment involving a cat and its attempt to defy gravity.

Again, memorable content is findable content. So, while not every site can emulate Google's success at *just working* the first time, every time (though they should most certainly try), most sites can dramatically improve their search systems by putting the framework elements identified in this chapter to work and using search data and usability test results as a guide for improving site navigation.

Sign-up

Spinscape launched its web-based mind-mapping application in July 2008, promising to offer a slew of compelling features to rise above the competition and make mind-mapping easy. A **mind map**, as Spinscape.com states, is "a diagram, or set of diagrams, used to represent words, ideas, tasks, or other items linked to and arranged radially around a central key word or idea." At its core, it's a method of generating and organizing ideas, collaborating with others, solving problems, and making decisions. But since mind-mapping is a new concept to many people, it's likely to raise many questions as users experience the Spinscape home page for the first time:

What can I do here?

What does this site offer that is important to me?

Users who make it past the first set of questions and feel inclined to keep going will have a new set of questions.

How do I get started?

Do I have to sign up? If so, how?

In fact, these are questions users have about many sites when they experience them for the first time. On Spinscape.com, these questions may be difficult to answer, even for those already familiar with mind-mapping.

Figure 5.1
Spinscape tries to tell us
what it offers.

Spinscape tries to tell us what it offers: "A visual way to organize your information online." It also tells us, simply through the presence of a sign-in form, that yes, we will probably need to create an account. But how does it communicate the level of difficulty we can expect to face as we get started? How do we create an account? How do we know the reward will be worth the effort? How does it explain the concept of mind-mapping?

The answer, as you might guess, is that it doesn't. At least not at a glance, which is how we need it. To understand mind-mapping, we must watch the video or access the So What is Mind Mapping? page. To learn about the feature set, we need to visit the Spinscape Advantages page. To move forward, we have to locate the rather inconspicuous Get Started link at the bottom of the home page.

But this is not how we like to answer questions. We like to scan a page and get as many answers as we can in as short a time as possible. Eyes darting. Unconscious impressions forming. What will Spinscape do for me? *Tell me. Right now!*

Spinscape makes use of just two of the six elements in the sign-up framework. It misuses another. It forgoes the other three. Tsk, tsk.

Description

The purpose of the sign-up framework is to convince visitors to register and become subscribers. Active members. Paying customers. Its intention is not only to address objections that site users may have prior to signing up, but also, and perhaps more importantly, to *entice* them.

The framework is composed of just six key elements, and while they may appear small and insignificant, each can be absolutely critical to success. Each one can mean the difference between losing a visitor and gaining a customer. The framework as a whole can mean the difference between a one or two percent conversion rate and a ten percent conversion rate. Thousands of dollars, or tens of thousands. Millions, or tens of millions.

The purpose of the sign-up framework is first and foremost to answer the questions that appear in the user's mind as his eyes dart around the screen. But its real job is to appeal to the unconscious, where decisions are made. To incite a visceral reaction just strong enough to make him crave this unknown thing. To give him just enough information to compel him to want to learn more. To grab his attention just enough to convince him to take action.

In essence, the sign-up framework exists purely to *persuade*, and then to enable a user to act on his new impulse to dive in.

Context of use

The sign-up framework applies to applications that require users to register to save, publish, store, or otherwise take ownership of or manage the content they create. These applications are often presented as stand-alone sites that visitors can access for the first time only via top-level marketing pages, such as the home page or a Learn More page. However, applications like this can also exist simply as a section of a larger site.

TurboTax and H&R Block, for example, require that users create accounts prior to using their tools for tax preparation. Netflix and GreenCine require registration before users can have rented DVDs shipped to their homes. Blinksale and Freshbooks require accounts before they can be used to create and manage invoices.

This framework does *not* apply to conversions in a commerce context, such as the purchase of a product through a retail site. For example, it is not necessary to register prior to purchasing a floor lamp on Target.com—in fact, it is never necessary to register on the site.

The sign-up framework is used primarily within the top-level marketing section of an application site or microsite, but can also bleed into the application itself (more on that in the Blank Slate section below). The marketing section can include the home page, a Learn More page, and any other public page through which you can directly or indirectly encourage a visitor to register (such as by highlighting the features and benefits of the application). It also frequently includes a stand-alone registration page.

Task flow

With regard to task completion, the sign-up framework is very simple. Typically, a user explores the home page and possibly a Learn More or Features page, scans any relevant (and short) descriptions, and at some point accesses the registration process. He then completes the registration form, is confirmed as a new member, and then begins using the application. An alternative task flow, as discussed in the Blank Slate section, is one in which the user can begin using the application before registering, only being asked to register after it becomes absolutely necessary to continue.

Elements

Following are the elements included in the Sign-up framework.

Value proposition

The moment a user wonders what a site can offer him and why it's important, the **value proposition** begins to offer answers. As designers, if we can't communicate the purpose of an application at a glance, we risk losing the user's attention, and *attention is one of the hardest things to earn*.

To quickly explain to a user what an application is about, the written word is one of the best tools around, but it's ineffective to simply toss up a paragraph-long welcome message, as few people read generic greetings. Instead, it's best to provide something short, catchy, and noticeable. To this end, a text-based value proposition should be a finely crafted elevator pitch for a very short elevator ride. It can be a statement ranging from just a few words to a sentence or two.

However, simply crafting an effective set of words isn't enough—the value proposition must appear in a prominent place where users are likely to see it, as in this example from Twitter's former home page.

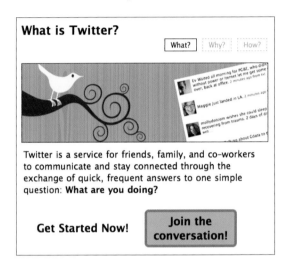

Figure 5.2
Twitter describes its purpose.

With just a short blurb, Twitter describes its purpose and implies the possible benefits of using the service. And with this text prominently displayed on the home page, it's easy to notice, so someone who has never heard of the site, or perhaps doesn't understand Twitter based on what they've heard or read, can quickly get a sense of whether or not the site will be relevant and useful.

However, Twitter's value proposition contains twenty-nine words—likely too many for the average drive-by visitor to process at a glance. The more easily the blurb can quell a user's concerns, the better. In this regard, Blinksale does more with less.

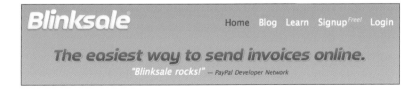

Figure 5.3
Blinksale does more with less.

In just seven words, Blinksale communicates exactly what it does and what the user can gain from using it. These words were carefully chosen, and each one helps ensure that drive-by visitors can quickly learn about the site. Specifically, three of the seven words in the statement—*easiest*, *invoices*, and *online*—are keywords that are vital to Blinksale's pitch.

Easiest. Invoices. Online. Everything a user needs to know.

Spinscape included a value-proposition statement—"A visual way to organize your information online." However, burying this site description in the header area of a design, within a long block of text or somewhere else, can greatly reduce a user's ability and oft-unconscious desire to notice, read, digest, and act on the information.

The key, as illustrated by both Twitter and Blinksale, is to ensure the value proposition is in plain sight. Front and center. What will Spinscape do for me?

Tell me. Right now!

Investment Breakdown

During a satisfaction survey run by a major airline, flight attendants handed each passenger a card upon leaving the aircraft that directed them to the airline's site and offered a nice incentive for filling out the survey.

While many customers started the survey, few finished, often stopping at a step requiring them to enter their ticket number (found on the boarding card stub). The users didn't realize they'd need this information and couldn't easily lay their hands on the stub when asked for it.

Many applications require the user bring something to the process, such as a customer number, a credit card, or a copy of their car title. When the application doesn't warn users up front to gather this information, it surprises them during the process, often causing them to consider whether it's worth the effort to continue. (This is compounded by their increased suspicion that they'll be surprised by more unidentified required information.)

In addition to needing information, users are often surprised when the application requires more time than they'd originally planned. Sometimes this is because the application requires more effort to learn and use than the user realized.

Users expecting a fast interaction suddenly are pressured because the application requires more time, which they may not have available. If the application doesn't set the proper expectations, an otherwise positive experience can quickly become frustrating.

Again, usability testing can help when designers pay careful attention to the expectations users form. Asking users what they think they'll need before they start the task (including both auxiliary information and time requirements) can help you determine whether or not expectations are clear.

Field studies can also help you identify the contexts of use. A team might discover, for example, that necessary receipts are unavailable because the user has already turned them in for reimbursement, requiring another validation method, such as online lookup.

In the context of signing up for an application, it's important to communicate what the user will need to learn and do to begin reaping its benefits so that she can gauge the level of investment required to start being successful with it. Here, Blinksale succeeds again.

Blinksale's home page features six small info-graphics, each of which reveals a benefit-slash-feature of the application. In the moment when a Blinksale visitor is deciding whether or not to become a customer, each of these blocks can help turn the hesitant into the self-assured and the skeptical into the confident.

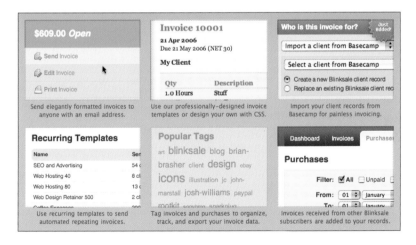

Figure 5.4
Blinksale uses small info-graphics to reveal its benefits and features.

Simply put, people need to know what they're getting into. So this second element—the **investment breakdown**—provides information beyond what the value proposition can communicate, such as what features exist and how they can be used.

While it serves simply to highlight the benefits and features of an application, what the investment breakdown ultimately conveys is how hard the application is going to be to use. If it looks like work, the investment will feel cumbersome. If it looks simple, the investment will feel light and easy to overcome.

Note also that this isn't *just* a breakdown of the user's required investment. Beyond the value proposition, this element provides a secondary method for communicating what the application is meant to do, so the visitor can understand it in more depth.

"The easiest way to send invoices online" value proposition tells visitors quite a bit about the site's purpose, but the six graphics that make up the investment breakdown get into the particulars. Here, users learn—in just six little blocks—that they can choose an invoice template, send invoices by email, import client contact information from Basecamp, tag their invoices, and more.

By contrast, TaxSlayer.com's investment breakdown is an example of how small differences in the details of a design can have a dramatically different affect.

TaxSlayer.com's investment breakdown appears toward the end of its home page. Using several small graphics, the site attempts to quell concerns, highlight features, and entice users. However, instead of stripping its message down to just a few words, TaxSlayer.com juxtaposes each graphic with an *entire paragraph* of text. *Tiny* text. Text that can barely be read, as seen in **Figure 5.5**.

What should have been one of the most persuasive elements on the entire Web site is now a distraction, a jumble of information to be entirely ignored.

For an investment-breakdown element to be at its most effective, it has to evoke a quick emotional and visceral response. It is not the time to wonder, If less is more, then how much more is *more*?

Do you dread tax time?

Is your receipt pile so big that you just don't know where to start? Don't worry, you're not alone! There are thousands of people feeling the same way across the nation. The great news is that **TaxSlayer.com** has a simple solution to your tax filing problems! The **TaxSlayer.com** tax preparation software is easy to use and gets your refund to you faster, so you can spend more time doing the things that you love.

We'll take you through it ... Step by Step

Our easy to use **TaxSlayer.com** tax preparation software takes you through your Federal and State tax returns step by step using our unique Interview Wizard that is built into **TaxSlayer.com's** tax preparation software presents the tax form questions to you in an uncomplicated, easy to comprehend format. Developed by our tax experts with over 30 years taxation experience, the **TaxSlayer.com** tax preparation software is supported by question-specific help and troubleshooting tips. It's just like having a personal tax agent sitting right with you.

Try It Completely Free!

We're so confident that you'll be completely satisfied by our **TaxSlayer.com** tax preparation software that we'd love you to try it out for free. No obligations, no contracts -- you don't pay a dime until you choose to complete the efile tax submission.

Support from Tax Experts.

We're not a start-up business who happens to have a great piece of software. **TaxSlayer.com** has grown from an established tax firm with over 30 years experience in tax preparation. Our **TaxSlayer.com** tax experts built the **TaxSlayer.com** individual software from our highly successful TaxSlayer Pro. TaxSlayer Pro was introduced to tax professionals in 1992. Adapting our software from the professional version means that you're getting the knowledge of professional tax experts built into your personal tax preparation software. You can use the **TaxSlayer.com** tax preparation software with confidence knowing that it has successfully completed millions of returns over the past eleven years.

Maximize Your Refund

The **TaxSlayer.com** Premium tax preparation software has many additional benefits, including a life events wizard, priority support and tax audit help. But one of the most popular features of the **TaxSlayer.com** Premium tax preparation software is the Deduction Slayer. The Deduction Slayer carefully guides you through the available refunds specific to your occupation, so that you completely maximize your refund.

Figure 5.5
TaxSlayer juxtaposes each graphic with an entire paragraph of text.

If there is more to know than what can be said in a small area of the home page, consider adding a Learn More page to the site and use it to feature a screencast or screen-shot tour of the application, with extended descriptions of major features.

Lastly, while telling users how long it typically takes to sign up and get started isn't necessarily common enough to include in this framework, it is smart, and therefore recommended as a best practice. Blinksale addresses this with the simple statement (**Figure 5.6**) at the bottom of the home page, "Start sending invoices in about 5 minutes!"

To potential customers, this means that even if they ultimately decide not to use the application, they will have only wasted about five minutes making that determination. Now, even five minutes can be a long time, but it

Sign-up for your free Blinksale account
Start sending invoices in about 5 minutes!

Figure 5.6
Blinksale reveals how long it will take to get started.

sounds like a small investment. In addition, many visitors will feel more comfortable when a clear expectation, such as this one, is set up front.

Spinscape doesn't communicate the time it would take to get started with mind-maps. In fact, it doesn't include an investment breakdown *at all*.

Testimonial

To leverage the principles of Authority and Liking from social psychology, which describe the natural inclinations people have to believe the words of respected authorities and people like themselves, SpinScape could have provided a simple testimonial or recommendation. A short quote conveying something positive about the product could have gone a long way toward convincing site visitors to become registered users.

The **Authority** principle reflects the very human tendency to trust those we see as being in a position of authority. A marketer, for example, may be more prone to believe a product is worth using if marketing legend Seth Godin says something positive about it. A usability professional may be more prone to buy a certain book if *Don't Make Me Think!* (New Riders) author Steve Krug recommends it.

In other words, simply adding a short testimonial to the home page from a known and respected authority figure can often inspire a visitor's sense of trust. On Squidoo.com, for example, the *New York Times* is cited as saying that Squidoo is "a home where bloggers can plumb those obscure passions." The *Times* is a highly respected source, so it becomes easier to trust the site.

Similarly, the **Liking** principle reflects our human tendency to trust people we see as being *like ourselves*. On Amazon.com, a customer who writes a product review can have remarkable influence over whether another customer purchases or avoids the product simply because the reviewer's name is Joe and he lives in Jacksonville. These facts remind the potential customer of himself, even if the demographic association is loose at best. (In fact, displaying the reviewer's name and location is generally more persuasive than showing the review alone.)

On Spinscape, a glowing recommendation from another designer or developer—someone you see as similar to yourself—could have helped convince users the application was worth a second look.

When a testimonial is used in conjunction with the investment breakdown and the other persuasive elements in the sign-up framework, it reinforces a user's developing belief that the application is worth exploring. If used alone, it can have the same effect, but it is likely to be less potent.

Call to action

Once you have sufficiently piqued the user's interest, you can use a quick call-to-action statement to tell him what to do next. A **call-to-action state-ment** is simply a short phrase, written as a command and worded to compel the user to take action.

When trying to convince a visitor to become a member, the call to action can be, and often is, created in as few as three words:

> *Sign up now!*

However, an effective way to get visitors excited about an application and build momentum is to let them move forward *without* requiring registration. You can instead offer a call to action that entices the user to do something tangible with the application. In other words, instead of *Sign up now!* consider a call to action such as *Create your first invoice now!* or *Write your first post now!* or something else.

The idea, simply put, is to drop visitors straight into the deep end. Enable them to *do* something as quickly as possible. Let them splash around for a bit before being asked to commit. This gives the visitor the freedom to experiment with the application, easing the pain of handing over his email address to create *yet another account* on *yet another site*.

An early version of the TripIt home page did this well.

Figure 5.7
TripIt describes how to get a travel itinerary.

To start using this trip-itinerary-sharing application, the user simply emails an itinerary from any major travel service (airline, hotel, and so on) to plans@tripit.com, and gets back a sample of a shared itinerary. And the user can do this as many times as he likes—the only reason to sign up is to *share* his itinerary with other people.

If it's not necessary to ask visitors to register before they get started with your application, then *don't*. Get them moving forward by encouraging them to do something with the product itself and ask for registration information only when it becomes necessary (this is often referred to as **lazy registration**). The simple act of using the application, in fact, can be quite persuasive—a user who has already started learning and benefiting from an application is more prone to sign up, and a registrant who has prior experiences with an application is likelier to be a more committed user.

Spinscape badly misused the call-to-action statement when it included the words *Get Started* at the bottom of its home page. *Get Started* should link either to the registration page or the application itself, but instead it leads to a page that simply provides links to a couple of tutorials. In fact, there is no clear way on the site to access the registration form. In using the call to action in this way, Spinscape set a false expectation, broke convention unnecessarily, and gained nothing by doing so. It's likely that this decision negatively affects the site's conversion rate.

It's also important to note that the call to action should not be written in the form of a question, but rather as a direct command.

Blank slate (a.k.a Immediate Engagement)

Of course, nothing offers a more compelling reason to sign up than a great user experience, so it's important to make sure that the user's first step is one that leads him into a five-star hotel room rather than off a cliff.

Many applications have what's known as a **blank slate**—a screen designed to be filled with user-generated content but that is currently devoid of that content, leaving the user wondering what to do next.

The primary objective is to walk the user through the answer to every question he might come up with. Ultimately, the goal is to make sure that the user's goals in any given moment are met.

Here are a couple of examples:

First is Basecamp, a Web-based project-management system that features the ability to create messages and to-do lists, set project milestones, and chat with other people on the project. When a new project is created in Basecamp, several of the main tabs feature a short screencast.

Figure 5.8
Basecamp fills its blank slate with instructive screencasts.

When a user sees the Messages screen for the first time, for example, his goal is to figure out what the page does, why it matters, and how to use it. To answer all three questions, all he needs to do is click to watch the video for a crash course on the value and usage of each major feature on that screen.

With any luck, the user's next goal will be to take action, so above each screencast is a large, red link that tells him how to do just that. To get started, the Messages tab tells users to "Post the first message for this project." By offering this, the user can click once and start being productive.

Without the screencast and large red link, he would be left with a mostly empty screen that offers no clues about how to get started. In other words, a *blank slate.* Your goal is to avoid leaving the blank slates blank by filling them up with useful information and entry points that get your users moving forward—things that facilitate *immediate engagement.*

The screencast and red link in Basecamp set the barrier to entry very low by giving new users a way to get familiar with the tool in just a minute.

The one caveat to this example is that Basecamp requires the user to sign up before creating his first project. Photoshop Express, from Adobe Labs, does better by offering a Test Drive button on its home page. Instead of requiring sign-up, Photoshop Express lets the user dive in without asking for personal information.

Figure 5.9
Photoshop Express lets users dive in without entering personal information.

Upon clicking Test Drive, the user can experiment with the application using preloaded images, so he can find out what he can do to the images he'll eventually upload himself and how the application can benefit him. No blank slate here—instead, the user can become immediately engaged. In less than five clicks, he can go from the home page to editing a photograph. He can sign up at any point using the Join Now button, and the application prompts him to sign up whenever he tries to do something that requires it. (Registration is indeed required to perform most tasks on the site, but users can experiment with basic functionality a bit before being asked to register.)

The key to getting the user moving is to give him the information he needs, right when he needs it, and then get out of the way. If he signs up for the application at this point, it's more likely he'll do so because he's confident he really wants to use it.

Registration form

Of course, to sign up at all, the user will need the last and most critical part of the sign-up framework: the registration form itself. Unfortunately, many things can go wrong in the moment a user tries to complete a form, and registration forms are certainly no exception.

First, a user can make plenty of mistakes. He can choose a user name already in use, enter mismatched passwords, skip a required field, forget to check a Terms of Service check box, or any number of things.

Second, a user with a half-hearted commitment to signing up can be deterred by a lengthy registration form, suddenly deciding it's just not worth the time or energy.

Third, a registration form with a tricky confirmation process can lead to confusion and end up frustrating the user. For example, many registration processes require that the user check his email for a message that is automatically sent upon registering and ask him to click it to confirm the address is legitimate. But what happens when he fails to notice the message to check his email? What happens if he gets distracted by a phone call or some other occurrence and forgets?

Registration needs to be painless. After having done the hard work of getting a person to sign up, the worst thing you can do is alienate him in this important moment.

When the registration process is designed well, it not only enhances a user's trust in an application, it can further solidify his commitment to using it.

To ensure a smooth process, first remove anything from the sign-up form that isn't absolutely required. In most cases, all that's needed is the user's name, email address, and password. In many cases, it's not even necessary to acquire the user's name (though it is a nice personal touch to use his name in newsletters and such later).

PearBudget, for example, requires only an email address and a password.

Figure 5.10
PearBudget requires only an email address and password.

If you need your users to build up more comprehensive profiles in an application, save this step for later whenever possible. Get them signed up first, and get the details later.

Keeping the form as short as possible lowers the barrier to entry, especially when employing so-called lazy registration, which lets the user start using the application without registering.

Additionally, since everyone makes mistakes on even the simplest forms, be sure to include real-time form validation so that users can catch and correct their mistakes as they are made, and make sure error messages are written to tell users how to do things correctly.

> *Your email address should be in the form me@mydomain.com.*

Surprisingly, Spinscape's registration form, at the time of this writing, is is quite difficult to find. It doesn't have its own page; it's positioned next to the sign-in form on the Sign In page. There is no clear path to the page, and the site's entry points often lead to unexpected places.

With just a few design tweaks, Spinscape could likely dramatically increase its conversion rate.

To learn more about the design of Web forms, there's no better authority than Luke Wroblewski, Senior Director of Product Ideation and Design for Yahoo. His book, *Web Form Design: Filling in the Blanks* (Rosenfeld Media), is the most thorough resource on the market. For information specifically on sign-up forms, see his blog post "Sign-Up Form Patterns," at http://www.lukew.com/ff/entry.asp?702.

Design Criteria

As you can see, most of the elements in this framework exist purely to *persuade*. The value proposition makes the application sound exciting and useful. The investment breakdown shows off the best features. The testimonial convinces the user that people like him or people he respects recommend it. The call to action compels him to get moving.

By taking a close look at what the sign-up framework truly accomplishes, we can extrapolate key design criteria to inform possible improvements and alternative methods.

Communicate a clear value proposition

First, as discussed earlier, our applications must communicate a clear value proposition. But it's important to understand that what matters is not the form in which a value proposition is communicated, but that it is communicated at all. The value-proposition element, in fact, is named according to its intention, not its design. In other words,though it's very often presented as a textual statement, such as a tag line or slogan, it doesn't have to be.

Figure 5.11
Hulu communicates its value proposition through a single button.

For example, noticeably missing from Hulu.com is any sort of text-based statement describing its purpose. What it offers instead is an auto-advancing slide show of television-show synopses, each of which appears adjacent to a button simply labeled *Watch Now*. A user who has never been to the site—who has never even heard of Hulu.com—can almost immediately deduce that the site enables him to watch TV shows online via a quick glance at these combined elements.

Allrecipes.com also lacks a value-proposition statement. There the value of the site is communicated almost entirely by the domain name itself.

This approach works best when an application has a single focus—Flickr is for sharing images, YouTube is for sharing video, and so on. The primary activity that the application supports can be communicated in a number of ways beyond using the written word.

Again, we're not advocating that you do only what has been done before—to simply copy successful sites without any thought to the context and purpose of your own application. Explore ways to communicate the value proposition without using a single word. If the scope of the application is focused on a single activity, then communicating that activity may be a relatively simple task.

Set expectations

One of the primary goals for the investment-breakdown element is to set expectations—to let users know how much work will be involved in getting started. Setting expectations is vital to convincing a user that the reward for taking action is worth the effort of doing so.

Figure 5.12
Senduit sets expectations without offering an explicit investment breakdown.

Senduit.com does an effective job of setting expectations without offering an explicit investment breakdown. Granted, it's an extremely simple application—all it does is provide users with a temporary URL for sharing a file—but the required effort level is communicated by nothing more than two numbered steps that contain a total of seven words.

Spinscape could set expectations by showing a screen shot of a sample mind-map—one that illustrates the value of mind-maps.

Demonstrate that it works well

Of course, because users also need to feel as though an application is trustworthy, it takes a little more than clear expectations to convince them to get moving. While a testimonial is a great way to reassure users, it's hardly the only way.

Leveraging the idea of **social proof**, the home page for BasecampHQ.com offers this statement:

> *Trusted by millions, Basecamp is the leading Web–based project collaboration tool.*

Trusted. By. Millions.

This statement encourages the user to believe, at least subconsciously, that if millions of users trust it, then surely some of those people are like the user—in the same situation, with similar needs—and that some of them are bound to be people the user can respect or admire or trust, so it must be a decent application.

Also, by letting users experiment with an application prior to signing up—by providing a method for immediate engagement—they can see for themselves that it works well (assuming, of course, that it *does* work well). No special design elements required.

Encourage action and enable progress

Hulu's Watch Now button is a one-click call to action composed of just two words against a faux–3-D button graphic. It couldn't be simpler. It also couldn't be more effective.

The call to action most often is a button—or is at least positioned *next* to a button. In addition to a button's text label, though, part of what makes this solution enticing are the **affordances** (attributes of a design that implicitly suggest how it is to be used) a button communicates by way of its faux–3-D appearance. The drop shadow. The gradient that makes it look tactile.

On many start pages—customizable home pages such as My Yahoo— modules can be dragged and dropped to organize the content on the page. On iGoogle, for example, rolling over the title bar of a module results in the display of an icon version of the *move* cursor, indicating that the module can be dragged. Design details like these are key to showing a user what can be done and how to do it, and affordances are used in the context of start pages to compel a user to begin customizing his page. You can apply this idea to the first steps of application usage in much the same way.

Beyond encouraging the user to take action, however, it's important to enable him to take *productive* actions. The act of signing up is a barrier—it's not part of using an application and it doesn't lead the user to the results of his efforts. It doesn't help him see the value of the application. Instead, consider applying the idea of immediate engagement by letting the user use the application before you ask them to hand over personal information.

Associate the user to the user's actions

You may have noticed that the examples we've offered in this section so far are not the kinds of applications the sign-up framework applies to—they are not walled gardens for which a user must register in order to create or use data. This is because, frankly, not every application that currently requires registration actually *needs* to.

A registration form asks a user to supply his name, email address, and possibly other information to create a unique database entry that intrinsically couples the user to his actions and content. It doesn't have to be done this way.

Figure 5.13
Drop.io foregoes the need for registration.

Drop.io, another file-sharing application, forgoes the need for registration despite the variety of features it offers that enable users to manage files. To create a storage area for shared files, you simply choose a keyword to use in a custom URL (drop.io/keyword). No email address required. A password can be created if the shared files need to be protected, but it is optional.

And to use TripIt for the first time, you simply forward a travel confirmation email to receive a sample TripIt itinerary. Building on this idea, an application could simply use the email address to auto-create an account for the user so he can effectively sign in later on, and perhaps create a password. An email address is perfect as a unique database identifier, and a password is all that's needed to protect an account, so an application could limit what it asks for to these two things, and ask people to provide more information *over time*. Aside from decreasing the initial investment of getting started, this process can gradually reinforce a user's commitment to the application. (People tend to strongly prefer to stay consistent with their own prior actions, so in theory, the more actions a user takes toward building a profile and establishing a history on a specific site, the more committed to it the user becomes.)

One of the least tapped areas of exploration in application design is that of nonstandard ways to couple users with their actions. Ask yourself, Can we use something other than a form? Do we really need more than a single piece of information to create a database entry for the user? And does the process of coupling a user to his data have to be separate from core-application task flows, or can we present it more organically?

If you can acquire a user's profile information through actual usage of the application, instead of by sending him through a stand-alone process that has nothing to do with its use (such as a registration form), you reduce the user's initial investment. As such, the user no longer has to *decide* to sign up—the user essentially "signs up" the moment he takes action on the site.

On sites where registration is necessary, most of the elements in this framework are essential; you should include, at a minimum, the value proposition, call to action, registration form, and at least one of the other elements.

However, a system designed to create a user account without an explicit registration process can achieve its conversion goals *without* this last piece of the sign-up framework. Signing up can then become a natural, organic process that results from regular use.

Imagine that.

The web without registration forms.

About Us

At this point in web history, few people haven't heard of Amazon, but suppose for a moment that you are one of them. Or that despite your familiarity with the site, you are interested in learning about how the company got started, what it hopes to achieve in the coming years, or whether or not it's involved in any charitable activities. To do this, you look for a link labeled About Us, or something similar.

On Amazon.com, you don't find it.

The site offers financial info, press releases, corporate governance, contact methods, and more, but you'll have to try hard to find anything at all on the company's backstory, culture, mission, and so on. In fact, this content does exist, but it's found on the Careers page, so you may only find it if you're looking for a job. And, strangely, there is far more information available about Amazon on Wikipedia than there is on Amazon's own site.

So with no information, will you trust the site? Can you be sure that Amazon is a reputable company and that your order will arrive? Can you trust the company with your credit card information?

It may seem trivial to document something so common and obvious, but the About Us framework shows the value of looking beyond design patterns and exploring interaction design frameworks. While About Us sections are found on most websites, no pattern library we've seen has documented it. And there are important questions to be asked:

What information should be included?

What makes the information important?

What user need does it meet?

Where and how is this content used?

Just like any other framework, About Us works to achieve specific goals, and its seemingly mundane chunk of content has just as much room for innovation as anything else. Understanding these goals is key to reinventing the way About Us works for your oganization.

Description

About Us doesn't always literally mean about *us*—the framework just as easily and commonly applies to individuals as organizations. In fact, About Us can be found in some form on just about every site type there is, from corporate sites to walled-garden web applications, from giant retailers to hobbyist bloggers. If a person has anything at all to say, and puts it online, an About Us section helps visitors learn more and begin to trust the site.

As with all the other frameworks in this book, we'll start by taking a look at what About Us is and what it does right now, we'll pull design criteria from it, and then we'll explore some possibilities for achieving the framework's goals in different ways.

As we've said, About Us is a trust builder. It is not, however, generally used as a *primary* trust builder—that's better left to the rest of the site. A retail company's shopping experience, promptness of delivery, quality of customer service, and follow-up have a far bigger impact on user trust than anything About Us could possibly offer. But it can help establish an initial sense of reliability and competence, and simply let users know there's an actual company or person behind the site. It makes the inhuman human. To that end, it's worthy of a second look, and could certainly benefit from some fresh ideas.

Context of use

Users typically read About Us when they want to know more about a site, often during their first few visits. Users turn to it when they want to contact the organization for some reason in person—via phone or by physically visiting the company, whether for customer support, to make recommendations, or simply to ask a question. (This can occur at any point during the life of a user's relationship with a site.)

Task flow

Users can usually access About Us via the persistent, or global, navigation of a site. It's frequently found in the header area alongside things such as the Sign In/Out option and My Account link, or perhaps even links to Help, site tour, and features pages. It's also commonly found in the footer, alongside other persistent links. Well-established brands such as Best Buy and Macy's, for example, bury their About Us entry points down at the bottom of their page templates.

About Us may span several pages or it may be just a single page that contains only high-level information. Merrill Lynch's About Us section, for example, includes quite a few pages, covering a range of information from a company overview to quick financial facts.

Figure 6.1
Merrill Lynch includes multiple subsections in its About Us section. As a company for whom trust is extremely important, that's a smart decision.

Regardless, About Us usually lives within the top-level marketing section of a site's architecture so that users can quickly access this information when they first enter a site, whether because they're unfamiliar with the site owner or because they need or want more information about the company or individual.

Users simply click the About Us link (or one with a similar label, such as About or About [Company Name]), wherever it may live, to visit the About Us page or section.

Elements

Following are the elements included in the About Us framework.

The company story

Collectively, the pages of About Us comprise the story behind a company or individual—one that, at least partially, shapes a user's feeling and perspective about that person or organization.

Many About Us sections start with an overview of a company or a site owner's biography—something friendly enough for media write-ups, but comprehensive enough to capture, in a nutshell, what makes the person or company worth paying attention to.

Imagine, for example, a scenario in which you want to purchase a digital metronome with a headphone jack and a secondary tone for accented downbeats. A friend tells you about a site that offers one. You've never heard of the site or the company behind it, and upon visiting the site for the first time, you discover that it indeed offers exactly what you want, but you wonder how much you can trust the company with your credit card information and whether or not the order and delivery process will meet your needs.

To learn more, you click over to the About Us page. There, you find out that the site belongs to a privately owned retail store in Boston, Massachusetts. According to the company overview, the store opened in 1976, is owned by Chelsea and Brian Craig, carries a variety of musical instruments as well as songbooks, offers musical lessons, and donates to the neighborhood high school's music program. The page also offers the store's physical address and a phone number you can call to speak directly to store employees.

From here, you may feel compelled to seek out discussions about the store on Yelp.com or through other means, but being the benefit-of-the-doubt kind of person you are, you decide this description is sufficiently believable and decide to give the store a chance. After all, you need the metronome for class on Monday so you can work with your students on tightening up their sense of rhythm.

Between the store's background story and the assurances elsewhere on the site that shipments always go out within 24 hours and can be rushed to you for a small additional shipping fee, you're satisfied enough to carry on. You add the metronome to your cart and complete your purchase.

Imagine, also, a very different situation where the site features no back-story. No address. No phone number. No donations to the high school music program.

What do you do in this second situation to determine the trustworthiness of the site? Perhaps you look it up on Yelp. Perhaps you Google the company name to see if anyone else has discussed the store. Maybe you post a message on Facebook to see if any of your music-teacher friends have bought from the company before.

More likely, you decide all this work just isn't worth the effort and instead Google the name and model number of the metronome, which you now know because you found it on the first site.

About Us offers a shortcut. Instead of scouring the web for information, we start to trust the company by believing what it has to say about itself. Instead of hunting for second opinions, we let the fact that the store donates to the local high school appeal to our good natures and decide the store must be worth our trust. A well-composed overview can go a long way. The more persuasive the story, the more persuaded we tend to become.

But the company story is not always as simple as a short overview. Through the About Us sections of name-brand sites, for example, we can learn about a company's business creed, goals, history, and much more, and this can take up far more than a single page.

Even after drilling down into the Our History section of Target.com—one of many sections in the About Target area of the site—it takes several pages just to tell the story of how Target became Target, how it made its mark in the retail world, and how its tradition of community involvement developed.

Figure 6.2
Target's story includes a customer-oriented mission statement and company history, but also information on how Target gives back to its neighboring communities, innovates the shopping experience, and puts an emphasis on great design.

The About Target section contains subsections about the company's mission, community outreach, focus on design, stores, culture, efforts to minimize its environmental impact, awards, corporate responsibility, and partners, and each of these sections spans several more pages. The Target story, and the company's commitment to telling it, is large enough that it spans at least a couple dozen pages of information.

Financial status

Notice also that Target's About section offers a subsection called Investors, aimed at people who have a stake in the company's financial stability and future. This section is usually specific to public companies because they are required to make financial information available, but it can also appear on sites for private companies or organizations actively seeking funding.

An example of a public company's financial section is the Investor Relations section of TimeWarner.com.

Figure 6.3
Note that the links in the main content area of Time Warner's financial section are exactly the same as the items in the sidebar menu, with simply a line of additional detail.

This single screenshot can hardly detail the intricacy and scope of a financial section, but it does offer a glimpse into what types of information might be included. Time Warner's Investor Relations section, as you can see, offers the subsections Reports and SEC Filings, Stock and Debt Securities Information, Events and Presentations, Shareholders Services, and Corporate Governance.

The decisions behind what does and doesn't get displayed in the Financial section alone are complicated enough that we considered presenting it as its own framework, but we've opted to spare you the gory details. It should be noted, though, that a financial section is another kind of trust builder. People considering buying stock in a company, spending a substantial amount of money on a provided service, or even ordering a digital metronome can use the financial information on a site to determine the trustworthiness of the organization.

When funding the construction of a new building, for example, you have only one shot to get it right, so hiring the right architecture firm and builder is crucial. Potential clients will seek out as much useful information as possible to maximize the odds of success. A section on a firm's financial status can help quell concerns about its viability and how likely it is to stay in business long enough to finish the project.

In Chapter 7, an example of a niche-specific framework illustrates how to identify frameworks within your own industry or even just within your organization. The financial-status aspect of About Us could easily be one such framework. If you work for a public company, consider exploring the financial section of your company's site to identify the elements it has in common with other public companies, what things are different and why, and what user-needs these elements serve to meet. By understanding the purpose and benefits of the section, you may be able to imagine more effective ways to communicate the information and do a better job of building trust for stakeholders.

Client list

Service companies, such as consulting companies and vendors, often provide a client list. The client list is not always within About Us—sometimes it is its own section—but we think this information still falls under the About Us framework.

The client list is *entirely* about trust building. There is no other purpose for displaying this information than to encourage potential clients to trust that you can do, and have already done, good work for reputable companies. These clients can be used as references, testimonials can be displayed as social proof of the quality of a vendor's work, and a healthy client list can even convince investors of a company's merits.

Many client lists are simply that—lists of client names. However, a client list's persuasiveness is far more potent when the list includes links to something that demonstrates the results of the work. For example, a client list for a web design firm that links directly to sites or applications the firm designed is far more persuasive than a simple list of company names. This way, site visitors can take a firsthand look at the firm's work and judge the quality themselves.

Happy Cog Studios, one of our favorite design firms, offers another great approach, as shown in **Figure 6.4**: its client list links to write-ups about the projects the company worked on, how the team approached each one, and what their responsibilities were.

Figure 6.4
Happy Cog offers project descriptions so potential clients can gain insight into their work and process.

Team profile

Smaller companies often offer a page of team member and management profiles. This profile, shown in **Figure 6.5**, also from Happy Cog, begins with a column of annotated head-shots, and extends into individual pages about each of the firm's team members.

Happy Cog's founder, Jeffrey Zeldman, is a world-renowned expert on web standards, but a potential client who had not already read *Designing with Web Standards* (his best-selling book on the subject), or had not seen him speak at An Event Apart (which he cofounded with Eric Meyer), or hadn't even read *A List Apart* (his must-read e-zine for web designers), wouldn't necessarily have that information prior to visiting the site. A quick read through Jeffrey's bio in the About section of Happy Cog's site offers the visitor a path to start building trust in Jeffrey's abilities and in the organization as a whole.

Figure 6.5
A team profile page gives a sense of the human beings behind the products.

These team profiles also help visitors develop a sense of who's who on the company totem pole by identifying which person holds which title. At User Interface Engineering, Jared is Founding Principal. At Peachpit, Nancy Aldrich-Ruenzel is Vice-President/Publisher. If you're talking to someone other than Jared or Nancy, About Us reveals that you're probably talking to someone who can't sign checks or contracts. But if you're talking to Peachpit's Scott Cowlin about marketing, you're probably in the right place.

Press releases and news

To further build on a company's story, many sites offer a running list of company-related news stories and press releases within About Us. Press releases serve to keep a site's audience up to date on events, management changes, and other announcements, while news pages enable a company to proudly spread the word about media coverage.

Figure 6.6
Posting articles from third party sources can reassure prospective customers that the company is reputable and that other customers have had positive experiences.

Zappos.com reposts articles that appear in magazines and on news and financial sites. The site has been talked about through many press outlets, including *Time*, *BusinessWeek*, *Fast Company*, and others, and simply reposting the content on the site creates a lasting way for customers and interested visitors not only to learn about the coverage, but also to enhance their trust in the company.

The obvious tendency is to exclude negative press, but as this chapter's Design Criteria section illustrates, there are ways to deal with negative press that don't entail *ignoring* it, such as by engaging in open conversation with customers via social networking sites and other forums. If the press coverage itself does not shed positive light on a company, the company can at least react in a constructive fashion and use the opportunity to address concerns and regain some of the trust that may have been lost as a result.

There is no particularly complicated method to display press releases and news articles—they are typically just offered as a list of linked and dated article titles. Adobe Systems, which, like many big companies, gets far too much press to maintain a complete collection, divides the home page of its Press Room section into categories, including Press Releases, Corporate

News, Product News, and Developer and Social Media News Releases. And it only maintains a list of recent articles, offering just enough to help customers build trust and get timely information. There may be no real benefit in offering a complete archive if all a visitor is likely to need is the most recent content.

Jobs

Besides encouraging a visitor's trust, companies also need to inspire confidence in the minds of potential employees. Job seekers need to know a variety of things about any company they apply to, including what positions are available, what's required to be considered for those positions, the benefits of employment, and even what the company culture might be like.

If the selection of available jobs is small enough, it can simply be offered as a list of job titles that link off to job descriptions and candidacy requirements. However, a large company with multiple offices, thousands of employees, dozens of products and functions, and a slew of layers on the org chart can't quite get away with a simple list of open positions. Companies in this league typically have to kick things up a notch and create a whole subsystem designed solely to facilitate job hunting and application processes.

To even list the available positions at Apple, the site's About Apple section divides jobs into two major types—Apple Pro and Apple Store. Under Apple Pro, designated for people interested in joining corporate teams, positions are then divided into departments, including Sales, Marketing, Operations, Mac Hardware Engineering, Software Engineering, and much more.

From here, you can click through to a category page (see the catalog framework in Chapter Three) about a particular department for a description of its primary functions, see what types of jobs are available within it, and then access a list of current job openings. Of course, once you find a job title that looks relevant, you still need to jump to the content page to read about the position in detail. And if you manage to find a job that looks right for you, only then do you find out what's involved in the application process.

But the Jobs section hardly ends there.

Job Opportunities

Apple Pro

Are you an experienced pro? New college grad? We're looking for the best. Explore the groups below for more information.

Mac Hardware Engineering
Join the team of ingenious engineering minds that design and develop Apple's revolutionary products. Mac hardware engineering looks for people with disciplines in electrical, mechanical, and specialized engineering, industrial design, and quality assurance.

Software Engineering
Make the move to Apple's software engineering team—and move the industry forward at the blazing pace of innovation. Software engineering is the division behind cutting-edge software like QuickTime, Spotlight, and iChat; the system-level software for iPhone and Apple TV; Mac OS X; and more.

Applications
Each Apple application is managed by a dedicated team of programmers, marketers, and project managers. Their passion for music, photography, and film is showcased in innovative applications such as iTunes, iPhoto, and Final Cut Pro.

iPod Engineering
This is team that delivers many of Apple's cutting-edge consumer electronics. The talented iPod engineers, project managers, and designers are driving the digital music revolution with products such as the new iPod and iPod nano.

Marketing
This team creates the imaginative strategies—in product marketing, marketing communications, and public relations—that represent our products to the world. Their innovative point-of-view is an integral part of the product development process.

Sales
The Sales team—including field and education sales, enterprise sales, the online store, and more—manages relationships with our resellers and customers. Our sales reps have the right combination of passion and product knowledge to deliver the Apple experience worldwide.

Operations
Operations' role is to ensure that Apple's state-of-the-art designs become industry-leading products, delivered on time and on spec. They drive Apple's manufacturing process as well as worldwide procurement and fulfillment.

Information Systems & Technology
These Mac experts use their creativity to design solutions for customers and ensure that every computer, phone, server farm, and network inside Apple is up and running, 24/7.

Legal, HR, Facilities
These dedicated, behind-the-scenes teams support Apple's global success. Managing everything from buildings to benefits, they make sure Apple employees are effective every day.

AppleCare
AppleCare provides award-winning service and support via an amazing network that includes self-service online tools, global service providers, and dedicated call centers. Their goal is simple: to give our customers the best experience possible, worldwide.

Figure 6.7
Big companies may need subsections within the jobs subsection. This page from Apple doesn't even show the complete collection of Jobs categories, only the Apple Pro portion.

While trying to entice job-seekers to explore opportunities, it's beneficial for a company to highlight the finer points of its corporate culture. Many companies, including Apple, forego this content, possibly to their detriment. Those that do provide it do so in wildly varying ways.

Office Max delivers its glimpse into company culture in the most bland and undramatic way possible—through three paragraphs of text about how the company is focused on people. That's right—a company claiming a focus on *people* used mere text to deliver its message, practically guaranteeing that the people it's so dedicated to are bored stiff as a result of reading about its commitment. It's hardly inspiring.

Adobe, however, as one might expect with all its design and multimedia prowess, delivers a rich and engaging microsite about its culture, featuring high-production video vignettes about life at Adobe, the top ten reasons to work there, its community involvement, employee activities, green initiative, and even its core values. (See **Figure 6.8.**)

Top *that*, Office Max.

So, once again, the Jobs section within About Us could be pulled out and made into a separate framework. But this notion only helps demonstrate how sites and applications comprise a whole collection of anatomical systems, and without each of them, the larger system would fall short, failing to meet the broader goals of the company and its users.

Figure 6.8
Adobe uses video to illustrate life at the company.

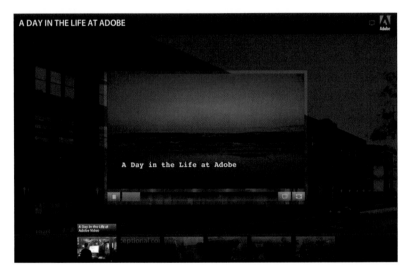

Contact

The final piece of About Us is by far one of the most important. Even Fortune 500 companies that are household names and offer no backstory in their About Us sections need to offer paths to contact the company.

But despite its importance, the contact section requires little explanation. Customers need technical support. Job seekers need directions. Vendors need shipping addresses. Potential customers need sales information. The list goes on. The only difficulty for any organization is deciding which information to offer.

A consultant with a home office will probably not want to list his address for all to see—he should hand over those details only when needed. But a phone number (for a separate business line, of course) can be helpful to people who might need a quick answer and can't wait for email. A Fortune 500 company, on the other hand, can have multiple offices in multiple cities and a different 800 number for everything from customer service to advertising inquiries.

Adobe's contact section, as shown in **Figure 6.9**, is far less extensive than its area for jobs, but still offers a good representation of the kinds of information to expect from the contact section of a large company.

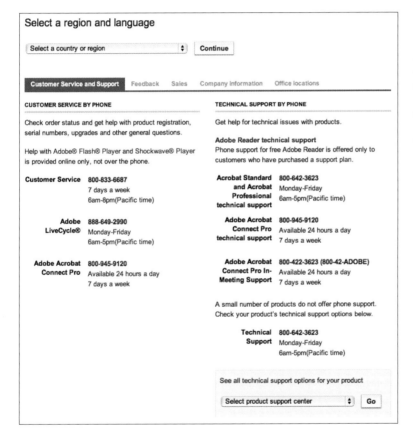

Figure 6.9
Note the "Select a country or region" drop-down menu at the top of the screen. Adobe has users worldwide and any of them should be able to find an appropriate contact number from the site.

Again spanning multiple pages, the Contact Adobe section offers phone numbers, office locations, paths to inquire about technical support, billing support, and sales information, and even lets users offer general feedback.

Another type of contact information—one usually given a larger and more obvious access point—is the *store locator*. (Of course, this applies only to retail sites for companies with brick-and-mortar stores.) This may or may not be included in About Us, but even when it is, a button is usually offered in a prominent location, such as the persistent site navigation, specifically for accessing a list of store locations. If it's a short list, the landing page can be a simple list of stores with their phone numbers, hours, and addresses. When stores are located in multiple geographic areas, users are typically asked to enter a zip code as a filter so the locator can list stores within or near the specific area.

Figure 6.10
Target's store locator lets you find a store with the department you need. If your closest Target doesn't include a pharmacy, the locator can find one farther away that does.

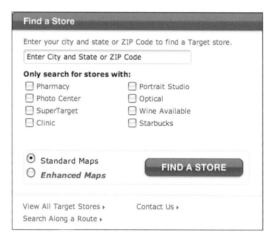

Because Target stores come in a variety of shapes and sizes and don't always include the same departments, the site's Find a Store interaction offers optional filters beyond asking for a zip code, so that users may locate only stores with portrait studios, pharmacies, photo centers, and so on.

However, designs that ask for more than a zip code can be deceiving; designers must be sure to communicate exactly what information is needed for the search to be effective.

Gap.com doesn't actually need the user to enter a complete address to find the nearest store, but it appears that way because its store locator page gives no indication of which fields, if any, are required. It's unlikely that there are so many Gap stores in a single zip code that the user can't determine the closest one from the results himself, so asking for an exact address doesn't necessarily help anything. Removing these fields would simplify the process and speed up the interaction.

(As a sidenote, Gap's store locator is also an interesting example of when instructions go too far. It's fairly obvious that one must complete the form and click a button to run the search, but there is a numbered list on the left that makes it look like it may be far more complicated. This can make users suspect that the instructions say something important, but since they won't be any likelier to actually *read* the instructions, this lengthy bit of text will unnecessarily cause users to doubt themselves and give up.)

The final type of contact method is, of course, the mighty contact form. Many books have covered the ins-and-outs of web forms, so we won't rehash the topic here. Just know this: whenever a contact form is a feasible option—for contacting customer service, inquiring about sales, disputing a billing issue, and so on—be sure to offer one in addition to phone numbers. It simply makes good business sense to eliminate the cost of phone support as much as possible when web correspondence will do the job. Internet service providers don't charge more for long-distance email.

Design Criteria

Despite the array of elements that can make up the typical About Us section, the framework only really serves a couple of key purposes. First, it helps users trust an organization, whether a small design firm or a mammoth megacorporation. Second, it facilitates communication so users can call, email, or visit a company; apply for a job without visiting in person; or simply keep up on recent press mentions.

But the limited scope of About Us doesn't mean there's no room to do things differently. Indeed, we can achieve the goals of About Us in different ways than are traditionally used, and we can do so more effectively.

There are two primary paths to mixing things up in About Us, and they map directly to the two things we've stated are the purposes of the framework.

First, we can explore new and/or better ways to establish brand trust. Second, we can open up communication lines more than they've ever been opened before.

Establish brand trust

Whether for a basement blogger or a Fortune 500 company, the important thing for About Us is that it helps users build trust. The company overview, as well as culture, team, press, financial, and client information all serve this purpose. About Us, however, could—and perhaps *should*—be reserved for delivering information and *not* used as a trust-builder, because no matter how convincing it might be, it's still loaded with content provided by the very company it's supposed to be about, which makes it inherently biased.

Fortunately, About Us is hardly the only way to lay the groundwork for brand trust.

Arguably, the best way to build trust is to deliver great products (or services), because great products generate word-of-mouth campaigns. Word of mouth is the most powerful form of marketing around, because people trust the recommendations of people they see as being *like themselves* far more than they trust the word of anonymous marketers with pithy metaphors designed to patronize as much as entertain. Customers who tell their friends and coworkers about a great product have far more power than most marketing departments can achieve.

The subject of how to develop a great product is well beyond the scope of this book, but we can say with the utmost confidence that great products are the best tools a company can have.

Imagine for a moment a product that you see as being *great*. Maybe it's an iPod or iPhone. Perhaps an appliance with an offbeat design. Or maybe a feature of your car that that you think is particularly nice. Because you like it, it's more likely that you'll tell your friends about it, and odds are that your mentions will influence their purchasing decisions later.

To exploit this idea, you need a great product. That's the hard part. Beyond that, though, you can take your energy off of writing riveting copy for the About Us section and, instead, put it into creating ways for your customers to talk about your products. In other words, instead of trying to build user trust yourself, you can let your customers do it *for* you.

Many online retailers support ratings, reviews, recommendations, and referrals to do exactly this, but they're generally tied to products the retailers themselves didn't create. A company that encourages its customers to rate and review its *own* products is in an even better position to earn great trust from new and repeat visitors alike (assuming, of course, that the displayed results are unbiased).

Of course, there are other ways to establish trust—in fact, the next design criterion could actually be classified as a *sub*criterion, because it has the same goal.

Open communication lines

The boilerplate collection of About Us content performs the simple job of letting visitors know whom they're having a marketing conversation with—who's inside the company walls, what the organization does, and so on—but in the Web 2.0 era, these sections are missing something that could be important: a list of how the organization connects to and converses with its community, such as through social networking sites.

As the authors of *The Cluetrain Manifesto* so aptly pointed out many years ago, markets are *conversations*. As such, sites can, in addition to identifying contact information, start pointing to the places where the conversations really take place—where a company's biggest fans and worst enemies can talk to a representative of the people listed on About Us. Where the *us* can talk back.

JetBlue Airways and others, for example, have dedicated team members to man their Twitter updates. Other companies should follow suit.

At Zappos, CEO Tony Hsieh is an avid Twitter user, and reportedly he encourages the staff to post freely about the company's goings-on *while they're at work*. Instead of banning call-center employees from using the web, as many companies do, Zappos encourages its customer-support representatives to talk openly about life at Zappos.

Figure 6.12
The important thing about this page is not the text of the biography, but the link underneath it that says, "Follow Tony Hsieh on Twitter." Zappos CEO Tony Hsieh communicates directly with his customers every single day.

And while JetBlue doesn't explicitly list its social networking activity on its site, the company is represented on Twitter, regularly using its feed to point out great fares, respond to customers who post about the airline, and even offer discounts.

Best Buy's Connect section points customers to blog posts, YouTube videos, and Twitter posts generated by its own employees, whether the content is related to Best Buy or not.

Figure 6.13
Best Buy lets employees throughout the company share blog posts, videos, and tweets with the rest of the world because, as the company says, "they have something interesting to share."

Another option—and one that's gaining in popularity—is for a company to create an account with Get Satisfaction (getsatisfaction.com), where customers can post any questions or comments they have. Other readers respond to provide answers or offer their own insights, but the companies themselves can also respond, adding as many employees to their account as they wish to communicate directly with their users.

Yet another possibility is to appoint people to read and respond to blog posts, forum questions, and other social network updates. Not only does this help a company listen more closely to its customers to hear what they want, what they like and don't like, and so on, it also creates an opportunity to address negative press and complaints. Through this open communication, you can acknowledge dissatisfied customers and give them avenues to resolve their issues. Of course, companies can and should also reply to happy customers—simply thanking the people who like a company or product enough to talk about it can build on the trust they already feel.

There's no grand trick to figuring out how to establish brand trust. Just put out a good product, be honest, fair, and friendly with your customers, and then give them ways to talk about their experiences, and a way to talk to *you*.

In the end, it's not really about *us*. It's about *them*.

7

Movie Sites

n this chapter, we take a look at a framework from a niche industry in an effort to show you how different site *types* can contain their own frameworks—ones you'll find only within that genre and that represent most of what sets the site apart from sites in other industries. Movie sites serve as a great example of this because, perhaps counterintuitively, while they frequently deliver fun and engaging experiences that appear completely unique, they are surprisingly *consistent*, and are therefore quite easy to pick apart and understand.

In the Design Criteria section later in this chapter, we'll look at possibilities for improvement and innovation. For now, however, we'll focus on the fun (and, of course, the list of framework elements).

Imagine, for a moment, that you've just clicked your way over to a movie site and begun to watch the trailer.

You see a man alone in the darkness, kneeling atop a metallic platform. White-hot sparks fly out from all around him. He is welding. You look closely at his goggles, searching for his identity, and as you do, he slowly lifts the goggles away from his eyes. His square jaw and enigmatic stare begin to build a mystery. Voices fade in and out. "30 seconds and counting." The echo of a slow, drummed heartbeat pounds in the distance.

"The eyes of the world now look into space." *Thump-thump.* "The eagle has landed." Your eyes dart around as you see more of the platform. It's but a small piece of what appears to be an enormous machine, the silver of its outer shell reflecting light in all directions. "That's one small step for man; one giant leap for mankind." *Thump-thump.* A countdown emerges from the noise, barely audible. "Six," the man says. It's already down to six. Your nerves jump. *Thump-thump.* "Five." The drumbeat speeds up. "Four." *Thump-thump.* Another piece of the machine. More welding. More sparks. *Thump-thump.* A man's deep and resonating voice boldly climbs above the noise.

"Space."

Thump-thump.

The countdown quickens.

"Three."

Thump-thump.

"Two."

The voice booms.

"The final frontier."

Thump-thump.

The music begins. You've heard it before. You know it well.

Chills.

You look upward and see the words written on the surface of the giant machine. It's the USS Enterprise. Under construction. The picture comes clear. It's the newest installment of the epic series of films and television shows that has served as the centerpiece of a worldwide cult following for decades.

You see the link to Facebook. You click it. You want to tell everyone you know.

You rush back to the site and step through the photo gallery. The panoramas. The character dossiers. Music plays the whole time, the mood swelling back and forth like an emotional tide. You download desktop wallpaper. Each click takes you to a new part of the ship. You are determined to learn everything you can. To hear everything you can hear. To see everything you can see.

These are the things that can happen on a great movie site. And StarTrek-Movie.com is a great movie site.

Naturally, this is all made possible by the movie-site framework.

Thump-thump.

Description

The movie site is a brochureware site designed to persuade and entice moviegoers into seeing the highlighted movie. Essentially, it's an elaborate advertisement—often so elaborate, in fact, that a well-done movie site is both experiential and informational, immersive and communicative, engaging and actionable. For most films, the site's only real job is to convince people to spend a little of their hard-earned cash on a night at the movie theater. For other films, such as *Star Trek*, whose potential revenue extends far outside the theater into toys, clothes, and other merchandise, it's to ignite a conversation so compelling that fans of the film will want to make it part of their lives, even if only for short time.

Figure 7.1
This support site is for the film *Shutter Island*

There appear to be just two major classifications for movie sites, which we'll refer to as "stand-alone sites" and "network sites."

Stand-alone sites, such as the one for Shutter Island, as shown in **Figure 7.1,** are exactly what the name implies—they are movie sites that stand entirely alone, like any other site about an individual product. A stand-alone site usually has a domain name that contains the movie's title (for example, StarTrekMovie.com), has its own home page, boasts a completely custom design, and includes almost nothing unrelated to the movie.

Figure 7.2
FoxSearchlight.com offers a collection of movie sites

Network sites, on the other hand, are nested within a larger network of movie sites and therefore tend to take on the qualities of every site within the network. Fox Searchlight Pictures, as you can see in **Figure 7.2** at Fox-Searchlight.com, serves as the marketing home for a handful of upcoming releases, and offers tools and content for each one from the same pool of options. On FoxSearchlight.com, every movie site includes some combination of content modules on cast and crew information, related links, additional content, news and reviews, and polls, all of which appear directly below an animated (sometimes interactive) Flash piece or marketing image.

While certainly easier than creating a unique site for every movie, wrapping a movie site up into a larger network of sites can be problematic, as the tools appropriate for one movie aren't necessarily appropriate for every movie. They can even result in poor marketing messages.

The network sites for *Once* (www.foxsearchlight.com/once) and *Adam* (www.foxsearchlight.com/adam), for example, at the time of this writing, are both part of the Fox Searchlight site. They draw from the same color palette, use the same labels, and have the same types of content. There's nothing unique about the two sites, even though the two movies are dissimilar from each other. Worse, since these Fox Searchlight microsites feature a module for auto-rotating content about other movies, the site for *Once* (a slice-of-life movie whose story line revolves around two musicians who work through their respective struggles by writing songs together) occasionally includes a trailer, without any heading or explanation, for *Driven to Kill*, an action film starring Steven Seagal. Unfortunately, this implies that *Driven to Kill* is what the movie company thinks *Once* audiences, as unlikely as it may be, will want to see next.

Also thanks to auto-rotating content, the *Adam* site sometimes features an ad for Musicians Institute, an ad that would be perfectly appropriate and relevant on the site for *Once*, but is not relevant at all to the movie *Adam*.

When movie sites are simply clumped together under a larger brand, vital experiential elements can be lost. Doing this turns what should be a unique and compelling user experience into a generic, and potentially very *cold*, attempt to standardize. The myriad attempts to standardize movie sites by Fox Searchlight result not in a compelling standard, but rather in a homogenized user experience that lacks meaning and context.

This illustrates that even with frameworks, you have to pick and choose which elements to use in a given project and adapt them to your needs.

Stand-alone sites are generally much more engaging. They are very often built using Adobe Flash, with which designers can better influence a visitor's emotional state through subtle visual effects, transitions, layered backgrounds, sound effects, and music (original scores, and songs from the soundtrack). These aesthetic elements come together to create a sense of immersion—to make the site feel like a *place* or a *mood* rather than a site.

People love to be entertained, and movies are a great way to make it happen. Movies can make you think, laugh, grieve, rejoice, and respond in any number of ways. A movie site's job is to convince its user that this film is the one that will give her what she wants.

To do this, designers generally avoid building them up into monstrous and complex applications—rather, they focus the scope of these sites so much that they typically break down into just a few very key elements. Regardless of their context of use, movie sites, despite all their richness and sophistication, are really quite predicable. And that's precisely why we've included a chapter about a niche—in this case, movie sites—in a book about significant web frameworks: to show you that frameworks are as equally discoverable and beneficial everywhere from the banking industry to the nonprofit sector. We only chose movie sites in particular because, well, it would have been very difficult to write such an action-packed description about a banking site.

Context of Use

Since we're talking about a complete site type here rather than an *aspect* of a site, such as a search system, the context of use is less complicated to explain. Simply, a person who has heard about a movie and wants to know more goes to a movie site to read the summary, watch the trailer, find out who's in the movie, and perhaps even collect an artifact or two. We'll talk about this more in the Design Criteria section.

Elements

Movie sites are a little different than the average brochureware site in that they need not just offer compelling content full of persuasive points, they need to deliver this content in the form of rich media. They need to sell their wares by way of multimedia adventures. Here's a look at the elements most commonly used to convince people just like you to eat a giant tub of popcorn, wash it down with a bucket of Coke, scarf a box of Junior Mints, put themselves through a two-hour emotional roller coaster, and pay for the privilege.

Splash page

In addition to its several compelling trailers, StarTrekMovie.com offers quotes from reviews, a way to find the nearest theaters and show times, a program for webmasters of fan sites, a link to a forum site, social networking options, and even an option to receive email updates. And all that is just the splash page!

Figure 7.3
The splash page for StarTrekMovie.com

A **splash page** is, basically, a movie poster with links. It can be as dense or as lean as any movie poster and has roughly the same goal: to entice people to find out more. To achieve this, it is usually filled with all the same advertising elements you'd expect to find on a movie poster, with the added ability to take action. On the *Star Trek* site, the main entry point is the large Enter the Site button, which takes you into the immersive Flash piece filled with animations and music, but you need not click it. You can skip the experiential aspects entirely and go straight to finding a show time, sharing a link to the site via Twitter, or becoming a "fan" on Facebook.

Splash pages are most frequently a part of stand-alone sites; network sites don't usually include one.

What's interesting about the splash page is how it attempts to achieve the goal of enticing people to learn more, as it's a truly great example of how aesthetics can influence thinking. While most of the text that appears on a splash page is rather blatant (for example, "In theaters on July 26"), the power of the page is really in its visual design—the mood it creates and how it can affect a user's reaction. Through the careful selection of just a few key images, or even a single image, designers can instill a sense of serenity, suspense, terror, nostalgia, or anything else, and a user's visceral and emotional responses are absolutely essential to making a movie memorable. Movies are all about storytelling, and the images used on a splash page are a designer's first chance (on the web, at least) to capture the audience's imagination.

Figure 7.4
The splash page for
Downloading Nancy

The splash page for Downloading Nancy (www.downloadingnancy themovie.com/), shown in **Figure 7.4,** offers the usual elements—the movie's release date, its title, cast names, and navigation—but far more compelling than this, it features two images, side by side. The one on the right is a photo of the film's two main characters superimposed on a computer monitor. It's not quite enough to build a mystery by itself, but when juxtaposed with the left-hand image, a mystery indeed emerges.

The image on the left is of a raised pair of arms, tied at the wrists by thick white rope. Written across the image in red are the words "the most controversial film you will see this year."

Together, these images create a mood—dark, if yet unplaceable. The text pushes the mood along, for sure, but even without it, the page as whole evokes loneliness. Desperation. An eeriness. A mystique.

The splash page's job, in reality, lies deeper than the obvious. Its job is not simply to provide users to learn more—that can be done relatively successfully through the equivalent of psychological parlor tricks. Rather, the page's job is to incite an emotional response strong enough that the user reacts to it and makes decisions. It's to cause the user to internalize the message. To make her feel as if she is there only because she feels connected to the story. That she is negotiating the experience on her own terms. That marketing and good design had nothing at all to do with it. Whether dark and somber or light and airy, the user's subconscious responses are what matter most in encouraging her to invest in the movie, emotionally and financially.

Ultimately, the movie site exists for people who want to know more. But once their web browsers are open, it's up to the designer to trigger the right responses. The splash page is the doorway.

Teaser/Trailer

As there is usually some room for experimentation and because not every element makes sense for every project, frameworks require designers to pick and choose which elements to include. Some are essential, some are not. It's up to designers to intelligently choose what to use and what to throw out. Keep this one, leave that one. Some elements can be excluded without any negative effect.

Trailers are not one of them.

As with the *Star Trek* trailer described in the beginning of this chapter, trailers on all movie sites have a nonnegotiable requirement to persuade. The pacing, flow, structure, and intensity of a trailer can have a huge impact on a potential moviegoer's impression of a movie. The movie trailer is on a level of importance with a photo when you're shopping online for cars (though a trailer is generally much more riveting). It would, quite frankly, be a serious error to create a movie site without one. Simply put, the trailer is the most important element on a movie site.

While it's extremely unlikely a web designer will have any input on the making of a film's trailer, she will most definitely have an impact on its presentation, which in turn can affect a user's overall experience beyond that of the trailer itself. Not only does the user need to easily access the video, she also needs to encounter it in such a way that it elicits a compelling reaction. The trailer itself has an impact, but so does the page that envelopes it.

Interestingly, few movie sites try to exploit this notion in any unique way. Many of them simply offer the trailer on the site's home page (presumably to make sure people see it) or on another page that has virtually nothing on it but the trailer.

While studying movie sites tells us that it's uncommon to place the trailer in a compelling visual environment, we think it's a very good idea to do so. Invoking visceral responses from viewers can only help establish the brand impression and reputation the designers are trying to achieve. It would be a shame to miss such an obvious opportunity to enhance that effort. Trailers presented against a backdrop of mood-setting imagery and effects create stronger impressions.

On the site for *The Hurt Locker* (www.thehurtlocker-movie.com), for example, a movie centered around an explosives expert doing the heady work of disabling bombs during a war, the trailer is shown against a still from the movie itself—a street clouded by a thick haze of dust, as shown in **Figure 7.5**. And this would be enough on its own to maintain the visual theme of the site, but the designers went one step further. As the trailer plays, unidentifiable object fragments float through the scene. It creates the unnerving feeling that an explosion has just occurred. The fragments could be burned sheets of paper from someone's private files. Crude drawings by a four-year-old child. A map from within a military vehicle. It's impossible to say. But since these fragments float through the scene the whole time the trailer is playing, what matters is that it can make the user feel like the thing being threatened throughout the trailer—an explosion—will indeed happen in the movie, which leaves doubt about the outcome of the story. Does the hero lose a limb? Does he die? Do his comrades die instead, leaving him to a life of grief and regret?

Either way, it's unsettling. This simple visual effect enhances the sense of fear and uncertainty that the trailer introduces.

If you're going to spend all that money making a great movie and a great trailer, be sure to spend a little more on the trailer's presentation. It has an effect.

Cast and crew

Cast and Crew is the About Us of movie sites. This section typically includes just the biographies of the people most prominently involved with a film, such as its stars, director, and so on. This information most frequently appears either on a single screen or on two separate screens—one for the cast, the other for the crew. Cast and crew information is less essential than the movie trailer, but because the list of people involved with a film can be a powerful selling point, it is by no means incidental.

That said, few sites seem to put much weight on the aesthetic of the information, and perhaps rightly so. How important is it, really, that a list of names that link to bios carry a movie site's theme as effectively as the rest of it? Probably not important at all. Still, cast and crew pages can be made to fit in nicely.

On StarTrekMovie.com, you can find cast and crew information in the About section, but in this case, the About section also includes the movie's synopsis (discussed in the next section) and production notes. More interesting, though, is that About is the only section of the site that takes visitors into the command center of the USS Enterprise, the most recognizable location on the entire ship for *Star Trek* fans. Somehow, this fact makes the About section a little more riveting. A little more enticing. Instead of offering just another list, this About section builds on a user's sense of place in the site. The About section is not a site page—it's a meet-and-greet stop during a tour of the ship (**Figure 7.6**).

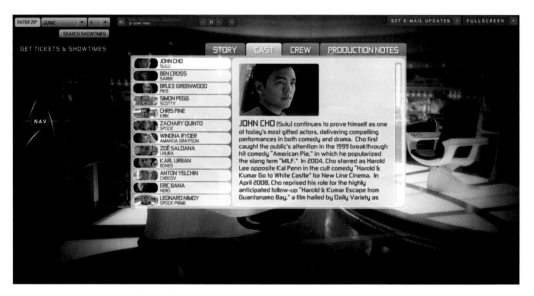

Figure 7.6
The About section of StarTrekMovie.com take users to the ship's command center

Synopsis

It's long been rumored that the elevator pitch for a movie (known as a logline in Hollywood) can make or break its production deal. If it doesn't sound like a moneymaker in under twenty seconds, it's probably not worth paying attention to. It has to be interesting. Compelling. Attention grabbing.

On the site for *Children of Invention* (www.childrenofinvention.com), the About section begins with this line:

> *Synopsis: Two young children living outside Boston are left to fend for themselves when their mother gets embroiled in a pyramid scheme and disappears.*

It's the only site out of the twenty or so we studied that really nailed the elevator pitch. On most of these movie sites, the synopsis was several paragraphs long and was written so that the entire thing had to be read before the real gist of the film could be understood. For *Children of Invention*, the copy-writer got straight to the point. This is probably how the movie got its production deal in the first place.

Figure 7.7
The *Children of Invention* site gets the elevator pitch right

The synopsis for a film is an essential bit of information to include on a movie site, because it works in tandem with the trailer to reveal the film's overarching plot line and persuade people to learn more. A user should be able to gain the same sense of story and theme from the synopsis as one who watches the trailer, albeit with fewer musical swells.

It's perfectly fine to stretch this out over a few paragraphs, but summarizing the story in just a line or two can help people quickly discern whether or not they're interested enough to stick around, and the way you treat users who leave can be just as important as the way you treat the ones who stay. The audience for movie sites includes people who watch a lot of movies, and movie-heads pay attention to cast and crew details, production companies, screenwriters, and just about every other detail that can be uncovered. It's important not to waste their time. A single-sentence summary of a film can be just enough to help them feel respected. Even if unconsciously, they'll remember that next time around. Positive experiences create positive memories.

Every site project should include a good writer. On sites where a specific piece of writing can be the single determining factor in a user's commitment, it's even more important.

Design Criteria

Despite the fact that StarTrekMovie.com is a relatively high-quality movie site, it does mostly the same things many others do. When you only have one job to do and you've already found a handful of ways to do it well, you stop looking for new ones. Many movie-site designers have, for the most part, stopped looking. But that's exactly where they fail. The design and construction of a movie site has been, in many cases, reduced to factory work, even though the industry is a niche that offers plenty of room for innovation. Many of these designers have settled on a collection of elements that do the job of persuasion decently well and have simply stopped digging for new ideas. In fact, it's as if there's just one group of expert movie-site designers out there building all of them, and they're getting bored. Apparently, even the excitement of working on experiential movie sites can wear off quickly when every new project has the same requirements as the last.

But if we take a look at the design criteria for a movie site, we get to the heart of what it's really meant to accomplish, and we can start considering new ways to do it.

In an exercise Robert ran during a workshop on interaction design frameworks at UIE's Web App Summit event in Newport Beach, attendees were split into four groups, and each group was assigned a different site type: finance, higher education, stock photography, and movies. Each group then sought out sites in its assigned category, studied them to identify commonalities, developed a list of design criteria based on what appeared to be the framework for that site type, and finally, brainstormed new solutions.

The criteria that follow are all the things the movie sites team came up with that day.

Establish and build a reputation

Job One for any movie site is to start building a reputation for the movie in conjunction with advertising campaigns. There are several ways to do this.

First, positive quotes from critics and media outlets (newspapers, magazines, and the like) can be effective, as they tap into the Authority principle from social psychology, which says people are generally willing to believe someone who appears to be an authority on a given subject. A movie critic's job is to judge a movie's quality and articulate those points to make a case for the audience to either see it or avoid it. Because of this, people assume, a movie critic is an expert on the subject and can be trusted, at least to some degree, making the critic a reliable source for advice.

Figure 7.8
Quotes from reputable sources can influence visitors

That said, many people simply don't trust critics—perhaps especially movie critics—because they so often disagree with their own opinions, which can in turn represent the masses. A slapstick comedy that entertains loads of people may not be highbrow enough for many critics, whose disapproval of the movie may stand in stark contrast to the sentiments of the movie's fans. Further, press quotes are inherently biased, as marketers almost never happily spread *bad* reviews in their campaigns. Finally, these quotes are often out of context of whatever larger piece of writing they came from (such as a full review in a magazine), making them frequently misleading.

So, while press quotes can certainly be helpful, especially when in reference to award-caliber films reviewed by sophisticated critics from reputable media outlets, they're not enough on their own.

A well-edited trailer can be extremely convincing, even for a movie that later on gets terrible reviews. But again, designers are unlikely to have any control over or input on the trailer. The only piece of the puzzle that site designers really have influence over is, obviously, the design of the site. The best things, then, that designers can do are to present the trailer on a beautifully designed page that sets the right mood, establish a theme that permeates the site design, and use their best judgment to choose the right music, visual effects, and backgrounds.

In cases where a film has a particularly noteworthy cast or crew, information about these people can be persuasive and should be highlighted in some way. A cast that includes major stars—reputable and well-known actors and actresses—automatically helps people believe a movie may be worth seeing. Reputable directors or producers can have this effect as well. Clint Eastwood, for example, is well known not just for his acting prowess, but also for consistently directing and producing critically acclaimed films. The simple appearance of his name on a movie site can be enough to make a user want to learn more about it. When people with significant star power are involved with a movie, a movie site designer is wise to put their names and likenesses front and center.

Figure 7.9
Highlighting famous cast members can be persuasive

Of course, no marketing trick is ever more compelling a motivator than a simple recommendation from a friend, and here is one way movie-site designers can step up their game. When you want someone to become interested in a movie fast, make sure she hears about it from her friends.

Enable word-of-mouth marketing

Another principle of social psychology is Liking, which describes the fact that people have a strong tendency to value the opinions of those they see as similar to themselves. This principle, in fact, is probably one of the core reasons Amazon has been so successful over the years—customer reviews enable users to gather the opinions of other people who have similar tastes or needs as themselves, and these recommendations have incredible influence over purchasing decisions.

The movie industry is no different. People love to be entertained, sure, but choosing a movie in which they will make a two-hour and ten-dollar investment requires more insight than the simple desire to be entertained. This is where the recommendations of friends come in. Word-of-mouth is the single most powerful form of marketing there is, and a single positive mention from a friend can turn someone from prospect to customer. Hence, sharing and networking solutions are incredibly effective tools. Strangely, few movie sites make use of them, and those that do tend to use them poorly.

The movie site for *Halloween 2* (www.halloween2-movie.com), as shown in **Figure 7.10**, for instance, offers links to the official Twitter and Facebook profiles for the movie. This appears to be a good idea until you consider how they're used. These options do nothing but link to social network profile pages. They ask for attention. What they should do is create a way to spread the word. Instead of linking to Twitter, the site could offer a prewritten message for users to post to their own Twitter accounts, such as "*Halloween 2* is coming out on August 28th. I can't wait! http://www.halloween2-movie.com." Users could then post the message to their own Twitter feeds and, with a single click, share their excitement about the film with all of their followers. This creates a point of investment for the user, makes the message viral, and requires only the effort of clicking a button.

Figure 7.10
There is nothing
scary about social
networking; it can help
spread the word about
a film

For users with blogs or MySpace pages, sites can offer a way to embed the movie trailer into their own posts, thereby sharing it with their friends and readers. Another option is to offer avatars featuring characters from the movie that users can download and use with their social network profiles. There are many possibilities. Most of them take very little effort to implement and have the potential for big rewards.

Robert's workshop attendees had another fascinating idea: they suggested trying out a viral print campaign. The band Nine Inch Nails once promoted an album release by placing clues (postcards, stickers, and so on) in public places, such as restrooms in bars likely to be frequented by the group's fans. This created an incredible buzz around the album, made those who found the clues feel powerfully unique, and generated a brilliant marketing story. Best of all, it shows that while the focus of this book is the anatomy of the web, the web isn't always the answer.

Engage them

Of course, even before convincing users to share their excitement about a film, movie sites must, quite simply, engage people. They must trigger emotion. Connect to them in some way. And once that's done, they have to leave users begging for more.

Fox Searchlight doesn't seem to get this. Content is presented in modules, and the modules are presented the same way for every movie on the site. They're in neutral colors to minimize contrast with the palette from the Flash piece. They appear in two columns, each module with a gray background and black text. Lots of it. There's nothing exciting going on here at all.

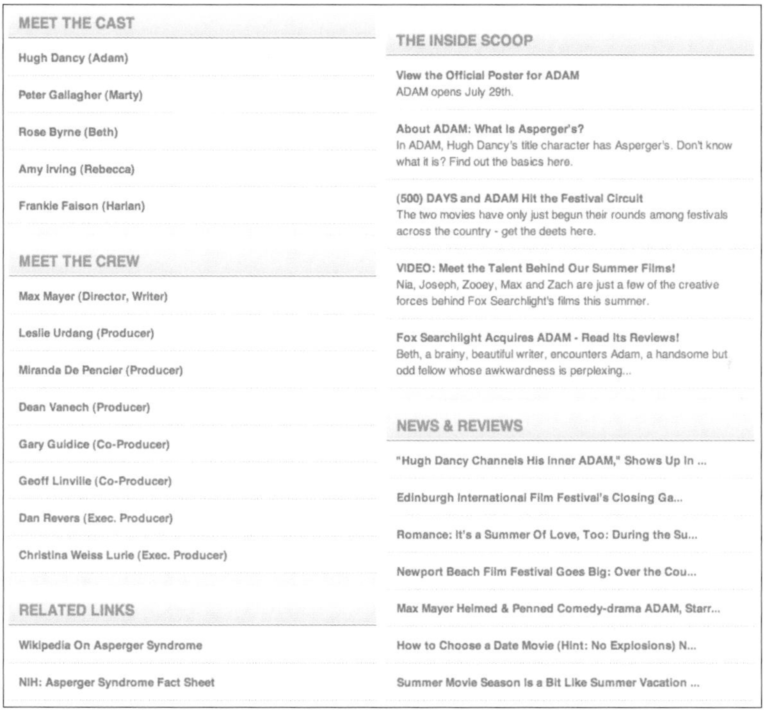

Figure 7.11
This FoxSearchlight.com content page is too generic to be exciting

The Star Trek site, on the other hand, is filled with mesmerizing imagery, visual effects, and a roller coaster's worth of musical ebbs and flows. There's a gallery containing over forty images from the film.

And not to be outdone, there are three different trailers, twelve television spots, and just in case that's not enough to build excitement, the site offers eight clips from the movie.

The idea is obvious, simple, and clear.

Build interest and leave them hanging!

Support lifestyle integration

One of the more interesting design criteria the workshop attendees noticed was that movie sites commonly try to create ways for fans to integrate the movie into their lives. Most frequently, this comes in the form of desktop wallpaper images, they noted, but this could be taken so much further.

Figure 7.12
Downloadable desktops
for *My Sister's Keeper*

Sites could offer the desktop wallpaper of the smart phone generation—wallpapers for cell phones such as the Apple iPhone. Avatars, again, could be doled out for social site profiles. T-shirts and posters could be sold. Visitors could customize postcards with personal messages and have them mailed to friends. Kids could print out coloring pages showing their favorite Pixar characters. Sites could offer ringtones. Just imagine the contemptuous satisfaction of having the Halloween theme play whenever your boss calls!

But where, you might ask, is the return on investment for doing all this additional work? For filmmakers, it's loyalty. It's the extra income from merchandise sales. It's the chance to build up the star power of the film's actors even more. It's a lot of things.

For the audience, on the other hand, it's far more. It's the chance to identify with something they feel passionate about. Something that helps define them to others. Something that enables them to daydream and live vicariously through a fictional character. To see the world, almost literally, through a different lens.

Now that's a user experience!

Thump-thump.

LOGO

SEARCH

PART THREE

Putting Frameworks to Use

PRODUCT GALLERY

USER ID

PASSWORD

SIGN IN

CONTENT

NEWS

NEWS

Building the
Framework Toolkit

You might never have given any real thought to many of the elements described in the previous five chapters. Others, you may have worked into your vocabulary long ago and never examined again. Either way, you may have missed opportunities. If you've never really taken a hard look at the design of a registration form, for example, your form's completion rate may be less than it could be. If you developed an approach to handling search systems years ago and never reexamined your opinions on the matter, you may have delivered search systems that fall short of their goals.

It's important to keep looking at interaction elements with fresh eyes, and we hope that our discussions of the design criteria in each framework have helped nudge you in that direction. But please don't think we're here to criticize. To the contrary, we're just as likely to fall into the traps of old thinking as anyone else. Simply put, it's incredibly easy to forget about these rote interactions and never put the kind of thought into them they require. And this happens for a very good reason.

Designers face a couple of recurring pain points, and they are directly related to each other. First, many find themselves designing the same elements over and over again. Contact forms. Search screens. About Us screens. Catalog architectures. Sign-up elements. Account management screens. With every new project, this list can look virtually identical to the last one. Second, most of these elements are incredibly boring. Worse, they take up more time than any other aspect of a project.

Is it that the state of design on the web is stagnating? Hardly. Every project brings on a new set of challenges, people, and things we can get excited about. Is the process becoming routine? That's unlikely, as many designers, especially consultants who work with a wide range of clientele, can work on hundreds of projects over their career and never see two that look even remotely alike. So how is it that these lists of elements to design look so similar? As it turns out, most projects actually have quite a bit in common.

On almost every project, designers make similar recommendations, at least in principle, about all kinds of things. Form design. Error handling. Global-navigation structure and position. Search placement and flow. On each project, designers adapt to the situation to make the details work for that project, but at a high level, trends run rampant.

Frameworks belong as a standard tool for design work precisely because it is so common for these rote processes to take over a project's time and resources unnecessarily, and because it's so common simply to chug through them without ever *thinking* about them. To this end, we hope the act of documenting frameworks will bring these issues back to life for you, and by paying attention to the rationale behind these systems, we'll inspire you to reinvigorate your approach to them, and to start pushing the boundaries to come up with new ways to solve old problems.

To do any of this, however, you must first understand how to identify, validate, and craft frameworks—whether generic or exclusive to a suite of products from a single organization—as well as how to share them to best leverage their benefits. In this chapter, we discuss these very issues.

Crafting Frameworks

As we mentioned in Chapter 7, Robert asked his workshop attendees to identify commonalities across sites from specific industries, document these elements, determine a set of design criteria for them, and then brainstorm ideas for how to put the criteria to work, thus devising new solutions. And this, in a nutshell, is exactly how it's done. But odds are, you don't have the time to arbitrarily choose a bunch of systems to document, nor do you have the will to carefully diagnose which sites to use as source material when identifying the elements that compose them. You need shortcuts. Cheat codes. Solutions that are "good enough."

Here they are.

Identify the problem

First, don't worry about preselecting a set of frameworks to document. You don't have to seek them out—they'll find you. In just about every project, there is a set of frameworks just waiting to be stumbled upon; all you need to do is notice them, and then flesh them out just enough to get through that aspect of a design project more easily and efficiently next time around. Each time you return to the framework, you can add more and more detail as you notice it. In other words, frameworks probably won't come off your fingertips as perfect, thorough, complete documents. Instead they'll start as vague lists, and eventually grow into a valuable resource, complete with examples, screen shots, and an inspiring list of design criteria.

To begin, you simply identify a problem that appears to need solving beyond your current project. The previous five chapters contain examples of this type of problem, but the possibilities far exceed the scope of this book (or perhaps *any* book). You'll find search, catalog, About Us, and other frameworks on countless sites. You'll design these things countless times. If you deal with it more than once as a designer, it's a good candidate for framework documentation.

While the frameworks we've described here will help you get started, our list barely scratches the surface (remember, we went into great depth for each of these; had we written up a total of just 20 at this depth, this book might never have seen the light of day). Here's a short list of frameworks you might encounter on a commerce project:

- **Account management:** Elements for managing a user's account—sign-in and sign-out screens and navigation; the Lost Password task flow; and screens to change or reset a password, update the user's email address, billing information, and so on.

- **User profile:** Outward-facing profile information about users within a social context—username or alias, avatar, list of reviews by the user, personal factoids (such as the user's location), and a list of products the user recommends or has added to a wish list.

- **Shopping cart:** Elements aimed at collecting and managing a user's purchase list prior to checkout—list of items, their prices, and the purchase subtotal.

- **Checkout:** Elements enabling a user to complete a purchase—total cost, shipping options, payment form, confirmation, and receipt.

- **Order management:** Elements for managing and tracking orders—shipping status, shipment tracking number, option to cancel an order, instructions for returning a product, and customer service contact methods.

You'll probably also need the search framework, About Us, an orientation framework dedicated to helping a user get familiar with a site (header, navigation, tag line, and so on), and, of course, the most essential commerce framework of all: the catalog framework.

As you work through a commerce site design, you can begin to document any or all of these frameworks as you think about the user contexts they support.

Tour for sources

Now, to validate your frameworks, it's best to study the work of those who came before you. Part of traditional design education involves doing just that. Composers study the work of other musicians, looking closely at how an artist put together and arranged a composition. Architects study existing structures to see exactly how they solved difficult problems.

Studying the works of those who came before us is a long and glorious tradition. However, because the act of designing for the web is still new, especially when compared with music composition and architecture, we don't have a formalized method for studying these works. Instead, we have to take *tours*.

Touring a site is different from just experiencing it. When you use an e-commerce site, you concentrate on your goal: selecting and ordering the right product. With a well-designed site, you'll be engrossed in the goal. You won't pay attention to the site's construction.

When you're touring a site, it's a different story. You can pay close attention to the details, from the subtleties of each widget to the overall flow of the application. The object becomes to pay little attention to the content on the site and instead focus on how it's presented and manipulated.

Finding the influences

Google has a policy called 20-Percent Time. Twenty percent of the time, Google designers can work on something other than their assigned project. The idea is part fun, part education. When you play with something outside your usual field of effort, you learn things you wouldn't learn otherwise.

Consider what would happen if we spent half that time—just ten percent of our workweek—touring other sites. In a forty-hour week, we'd spend four hours exploring the designs of other sites. If we spent four hours doing this every week for a year, we'd get more than five weeks of research done. We can learn a lot in five weeks.

What sites should we study?

We can start with our competitors, to see how they solve the same problems we're facing. We can also look at sites that have to be good to survive—where a bad design will kill the business. Companies that operate exclusively online, such as Netflix, eBay, Amazon, and Dell, earn most (if not all) of their revenue through the web. Looking at those sites can help us see how designs can evolve to meet the needs of both the users and the business.

It's not good, however, to look *only* at the most popular sites. You should spend part of your touring time looking at sites you've never heard of before. Jared and his team at UIE recommend to clients that they look at sites with very different purposes than their own organization. Banking sites, dating sites, universities, bookstores, and online utilities, such as blogging tools or artist-bidding sites, are all candidates for touring. From each of these examples, we cab see how designers have adapted basic architectures to the site's unique problems, and we can capture ideas for innovations in our own space.

What we look for

When touring, one thing to try to identify is what we call **problem/ solution pairs**. You can think of a finished design as a designer's attempt to solve a problem; by looking at the solution, you can often guess what problem was being solved. (This, in fact, is the key to determining a list of design criteria.)

The goal of touring is to compile a catalog of potential solutions to the problem you seek to solve. Down the road, when you run into a similar problem, you can refer to your catalog. You can also revisit the original sites to see if their designs have evolved further from your original inspection. Seeing how others tackle the same problems you have can give you insights for your site.

Libraries offer a great example of this. As described in Chapter 3, library sites built atop the Polaris system (because of design issues baked directly into the Polaris software) often deviate from even the most common-sense standards, resulting in poor support or no support at all for things that should be a given. Worse, other library vendors who build add-on products for the Polaris system have to adapt to it, often creating designs that only compound the problem. Library software vendors, and Polaris chiefly, would greatly benefit from looking *outside* the library industry to explore the standards long established by companies running successful sites that support similar activities. To put this in context, consider several of the ways a Polaris-based library site breaks from tradition:

- By inserting all item information into search-results pages, the system may require fewer clicks, but user scan't bookmark the content pages.

- By disregarding considerations for what types of content should appear in search results (which we discussed in Chapter 4), searches often result in a disorienting array of mixed results, few of which reflect a user's intent.

- With the default use of terminology such as *Patron* in site navigation, users are forced to think in ways not in line with their own mental models.

- Providing access to machine-readable cataloging (MARC)–format records (comprised of coded item information only librarians are likely to understand) within search results, and representing the MARC record with a book icon, which could appear useful to users, Polaris may solve a problem for librarians, who occasionally need this information, but simultaneously places right at their fingertips something users should never have to see.

A library catalog is functionally no different than a commerce site—
they support virtually identical activities. By studying Target.com,
Barnesandnoble.com, Amazon, and other successful online retailers,
the Polaris team could easily resolve many, if not all, of the problems it
exposes to its enormous base of library users:

- Creating stand-alone content pages that users can bookmark solves
  several usability, scalability, and accessibility issues.

- Revamping its search system will yield better results.

- Using terminology more familiar to userscould help them get oriented to the site and find the items, information, and functionality
  they need.

- Creating a librarian-only view with enhanced functionality would
  serve to hide content that is useless and confusing to users while
  still providing it to librarians as needed.

These solutions, and many more, could significantly drive up circulation
for a library. Circulation numbers are a library's version of revenue; these
numbers *directly affect* how much funding a library is offered the following fiscal year.

Observing within your own industry

For solutions specific to your project, also consider touring other sites in
the same industry or niche. What you find there might amaze you.

The workshop team Robert asked to curate a framework for higher-
education websites surprised everyone by noticing that the vast majority
of the sites studied were virtually *identical* in terms of information architecture and scope.

All the sites the group studied featured links to sections about the school
itself (campus life, history, and so on), academics, admission and financial aid, alumni, and the library. They even used identical terms for this
navigation. This incredibly standard navigation scheme showed up on
every site, from the worst to the best.

The similarities didn't end there.

Every one of these sites continued what Jared affectionately refers to as
the "girls under trees" phenomenon—the uncanny presence of at least
one photo on practically every higher-education site of at least one female,
frequently more, sitting under a tree.

Creating the appearance of both ample opportunity and appropriate circumstance, it makes us wonder if research might indicate that girls under trees are perhaps a major selling point for boys who would like to meet them.

If you work in the insurance industry, study other insurance companies' sites. Stock photography? Study stock photography sites.

If you work in the library profession, however, it might be best to stick to sites outside your industry.

Write it up

The next step in developing your framework is simply to document it, and we've shown throughout this book how a framework document should be structured. Of course, even this seemingly painless aspect has its complications.

While some managers believe that once a great design is hatched, a simple written document is all the development team needs to make it a reality, it unfortunately takes much more work to communicate anything but the simplest of solutions. Design deliverables are a critical bridge between designers and developers. Both the documents and the process that produces and delivers them deserve careful attention.

UIE once looked at how teams ensured they communicated design ideas successfully to their development teams. The research showed that teams can lose many important details as a result of poor design deliverables and a poor delivery process. The problem is compounded as the tools for interactions become more complex. As client-server interactions become more sophisticated and interaction capabilities, such as drag-and-drop, become richer, a simple write-up can't do the project justice. The most successful teams play close attention to the critical goals behind their deliverables.

In an ideal universe, the designers and developers would all go into a special room, put on special helmets, and within seconds have every detail of a design instantly communicated to everyone on the team. In our universe, however, problems occur because the developers can't read the designers' minds. It's not that the designers are deliberately keeping important details from the developers, but rather, that when you're neck deep in thoughts about a problem, it's hard to know if you communicated all the details in your head.

Here are some of the details that frequently get lost in the crossover:

- The priority of the different design elements: Not every element in a design is equally important to a user's objectives. In the design process, the team works out the relative priorities. However, if all that developers have to work with is a screen shot or a rough design sketch, the priorities are lost.

- Subtle interactions: Static images make it hard to show dynamic activity. It becomes more difficult when screen changes are triggered by users' actions that don't have corresponding visible controls, like a mouse-hover behavior.

- The rigor of the design rationale: In the design process, some portions can be heavily discussed and considered by the team, who will try out multiple iterations and hammer out the result. Once turned over to developers, changing these portions can upset a carefully tuned balance. However, other portions will remain unchanged from the beginning. The developers need to know there may still be more flexibility in these portions.

There are tricks to creating a deliverable process that gets these details across. For example, according to Keith Robinson, a former principal and creative director for the Seattle design firm Blue Flavor, the company creates a design-priority document that describes, in priority order, each design element and how it works. As implementation issues surface, the document acts as a guide to making decisions.

To help communicate the more complex interactions in the design, consider delivering an interactive prototype along with the written description. Many teams we talked to use prototyping tools, ranging from paper to Adobe Flash, to show the developers how a design works. These prototypes don't have to be fancy—they only need to show how the interface will operate when implemented. In fact, it's surprising how effective crude paper prototypes can be and how pleased developers are to have them.

One team UIE talked with used a visual language to communicate the designed features' varying degrees of thoroughness. The elements they'd rigorously thought through were in regular text without any indentation, whereas elements that hadn't yet received much consideration were italicized and indented. This simple yet effective visual language told the developers what they needed to know.

Other teams made sure they included a description of the testing process they used and the rationale behind the finalized designs. Communicating the design rationale, along with the finalized design description, can help the development team maintain the integrity of the high-priority elements throughout the implementation process.

Reducing development costs

In UIE's research, many teams had been plagued by ideas that looked great in theory but didn't work so well in practice. Sending the design back to the drawing board and the subsequent redo work increased development costs and slowed deployment. Finding ways to reduce or eliminate these costs is good for the organization.

Many teams turn to low-cost, fast-implementation prototyping tools to help reduce costs. Again, these don't need to be sophisticated tools—only something that quickly communicates the design's intent.

Having a working prototype is useful, but it's better when you have accurate use cases to work with. The teams with well-researched personas and scenarios, for example, found it easy to create their use cases, helping them validate their prototypes. By running the prototypes against the use cases, they could see where the design held up and where it fell flat.

When updating an existing design, a couple of teams UIE talked to used before-and-after images to help communicate the differences. Seeing the old design next to the new design, along with a clear description of the changes, helped the development team plot out their work.

Making edge conditions explicit

Alternative task flows should also be considered when documenting frameworks; teams need to clearly communicate the flow branches and edge conditions that could arise. Edge conditions are hard to visualize, however, making them an easy thing to miss when communicating designs to a development team.

Solid research is key to identifying the edge conditions that can pop up when using the design. Several teams established solid communications with the organization's support center, collecting up a list of the types of problems the support specialists were handling.

Other teams held "What could go wrong?" brainstorming sessions, to imagine what happens when key information, such as account numbers or hard-to-remember personal information, was left out or incorrectly entered.

Of course, many teams used usability studies to identify the types of issues that can arise. However, a few others used some novel approaches, including rewarding team members for helping to identify edge conditions. One team went as far as holding edge-detection parties, where team members competed to see how many different, unique edge conditions they could produce in a short time period.

One novel approach was the use of a "values list" to help ground the designers and developers on the underlying values instilled in the design. These values might include something like "We don't want our users to feel stupid" or "If we can avoid an error message, we will." Having values helps team members know when a little extra effort or resources might be the right way to fix a possible problem, instead of taking the easiest implementation.

One team produced a "Contingency Q&A" document, which helped them account for paths beyond the happy path. It posed questions such as "What happens when users leave the Headline field blank?" or "What happens when they try to type more than 60 characters into the Headline field?" Their answers went beyond the specifics and discussed the underlying rationale. (This would match up well with the values list.)

Getting creative

According to UIE's research, the teams that produced the most effective designs all had well-considered techniques for their deliverables process. They understood they weren't living in the ideal universe, and thus they dedicated resources to ensuring they communicated the design and its rationale to every member of the team. The results paid off with shorter development times and a higher-quality implementation.

Of course, the area of framework documentation most in need of creative thinking is the Design Criteria section, in which you attempt to reverse-engineer the motivations behind a standard solution, because this is the list that encourages innovation. When working through this list, consider the following comment from Scott Berkun (author of *The Myths of Innovation*):

Useful questions for innovators include:

- *Why is it done this way?*
- *Who started it and why?*
- *What alternatives did they consider, and what idea did their new idea replace?*
- *What are my, or my friend's, biggest complaints with how we do this thing, and what changes might make it better?*
- *How is this done in other towns, countries, cultures, or eras of time?*
- *What different assumptions did they make or constraints did they have?*
- *How can I apply any of the above to what I do?*

Many great innovators asked better questions than everyone else, and that's part of why they were successful. It wasn't genius (whatever that means), special top-secret brain exercises they did every morning, or even how much money they had. It was through the dedicated pursuit of answers to simple questions that they found ideas already in the world that might be of use.

Asking these questions should not only make it easier to figure out how something became standard in the first place, but also might prompt new thinking. This can lead to solutions that set you apart from your competitors and earn you some extra appreciation from your users.

Distribute the workload

Countless design teams have realized that a well-built design-pattern library makes the user-interface development process substantially easier; wrapping a framework library around it will help even further. A quality library means team members have the information they need at their fingertips. Choosing usable elements that work smoothly for users becomes the developer's path of least resistance.

UIE's research suggests one difficulty in building out the design-pattern library is the initial cataloging effort. It certainly takes a push from the library creators. But once it's completed, the value seems to be immediate; teams can start to discuss what works and what doesn't in current designs, laying out a vision for future development.

Like templates and guidelines, pattern and framework libraries require effort to build. However, unlike their counterparts, team members and contributors alike can distribute the work amongst themselves.

Because patterns and frameworks are more like standard engineering-design specification documents than a rule book, it's easier to get help to produce them. An organization that has already produced hundreds of web pages needs only to document the designs they've already implemented, thereby creating the initial collections. Over time, you can update the patterns and frameworks to reflect new thinking in the design direction and notify all the contributors of changes as they occur.

In the next chapter, we'll put you in the driver's seat and step through a hypothetical project to help you see how to integrate frameworks into your design process, when to start thinking about them, and how to make them practical. We'll even give you an example of applying design criteria to devise a nonstandard solution.

Putting Frameworks to Work

Like us, you've probably worked on countless projects that featured all the problems identified at the beginning of this book: vague requirements, limited time, few resources, low budgets, and tight deadlines. In this chapter, you get to do it again. This time, though, we'll do the heavy lifting.

Here, we walk you through a hypothetical project for which you are the interaction designer. We show you how to make use of and benefit from frameworks in these situations by stepping you through an example of their use in a typical project. This fictitious case study reveals where to introduce frameworks into the process, how to choose them, how to shape the collection of patterns to be included, how to use context considerations to drive design decisions, and how to leverage frameworks in the more innovative aspects of a project.

Design is an act of critical thinking; it is not the result of pouring ideas through a funnel of checklists. Hence, along the way we also offer insights into the meaning and importance of context, significant usability issues, and considerations to be made with regard to the design of any website or application, as these things must be understood to use frameworks effectively—and indeed to create *any* effective web solution.

The Setup

A client calls to ask you to design a travel guide site. Essentially, users will specify a few preferences about a trip, and as a result, receive a travel guide containing recommendations for hotels, restaurants, entertainment, and even places or ways to exercise during the trip. The client has a well-defined goal for the site, but little sense of how to achieve it. Further, the budget is low and the deadline tight. She wants to waste no time at all.

A few conversations about the project later, there are just a few important facts to pay attention to, and they resemble dozens of other projects you've worked on in the past:

- The exciting part of the design effort accounts for only about twenty percent of the project. The other eighty percent comprises the essentials (we'll talk more about that in a moment).

- The front-end developer on the project is someone you've worked with before, so you know her abilities well, and you know what she needs from you to get the job done on time.

- The sexy part of the project—the innovative part—is the only part the client really cares about. Any talk about other areas of the site quickly lose her interest and attention, which are, of course, two things you need to complete the project with any confidence.

- The team includes one interaction designer (you), one front-end web developer, one back-end web developer, one visual designer, and one eager, underfunded client. This is your team.

- You have extremely little time to get the job done.

Your job is to scope out the project, devise an information architecture, establish a task flow for the core interaction (configuring a travel guide), plan the navigation, and create wireframes for the whole site.

You have just a few short days to do all of this.

What's your first move?

You cut things out of the list. Instead of plotting out the architecture in a separate deliverable, you decide to go straight to creating wireframes and try to shape it from the inside out. And instead of creating wireframes for every page, you decide to focus on the core interaction and leave the team with a set of guidelines for anything left undone.

Building with Frameworks

As you probably know quite well, defining the requirements for a project isn't always as simple as asking the client outright. Your client has a clear goal, but she has few ideas beyond that. It's up to you to suss out what needs to exist, where to put it, how it will work, and why. Fortunately, this is one of the ways you can use frameworks to jump-start a design project.

While it may be impossible to know exactly what a commerce site, for example, needs to focus on and how to feature products until you're well into the process and have better client and user feedback, just about every commerce system out there is made up of a few subsystems:

- a catalog architecture
- a search system
- a shopping cart
- a checkout process
- an order-management framework
- an About Us section

Even without knowing what products a commerce site will sell, you could start designing its architecture and devising lo-res, generic page layouts. From there, as the requirements become more defined, you could simply tweak and shape the rough designs into exactly what's needed for the project. There's no reason to wait until every question has been asked and answered; as long as you know the type of site you'll be creating, often you can put together rough layouts without even knowing the site's eventual purpose.

That said, although frameworks are a remarkably effective tool for getting you started, if design was really this simple, the web would be virtually free of usability issues. Clearly, that's far from true. Once we get to the point of picking frameworks and design patterns and ironing out the details, the hard decisions begin, because this is where *context* becomes the most important consideration of the project.

Putting context into context

To better understand context, it's important to understand the three underlying elements of how an interface works:

- User: If you substitute one user with another, you would get different results.

- Interface: If you substitute the interface, you'd also get different results.

- Context: These are the attributes independent of the specific user and tool.

When usability problems arise in a design, it's often because design team members don't know something they should know about their users' possible contexts. A team with a strong awareness of these contexts is more likely to produce a design that will consistently delight users.

Imagine two different contexts for the same user and interface: a hypothetical user named Janice needs to produce a presentation with a PowerPoint-like tool.

In Context No. 1, Janice is creating a complex business chart in a presentation for the board of directors. The presentation is six weeks from now. She has never used the tool before.

To succeed, she'll need to ensure the chart communicates the content effectively, so she'll spend time exploring the tool's graphics-editing options, making sure she comes up with just the right layout and formatting. And because she has six weeks until the presentation, she'll pay close attention to particular details, such as fonts, colors, and spacing, so she makes the best impression possible.

In Context No. 2, Janice is creating a complex business chart in a presentation for the board of directors. The presentation is in 45 minutes. She's never used the tool before. To succeed in this case, Janice still needs to ensure the chart communicates the information as effectively as possible, but because she has extremely little time to craft a solution, she's going to rely on premade templates. She needs to choose a template that will suit her needs quickly, so she can spend the bulk of her time making sure the data is accurate. The layout needs to take care of itself.

In both of these contexts, Janice is exactly the same person. The tool is exactly the same tool. It's the context that changes the results of what Janice produces with the tool.

Buying a mortgage

One of UIE's clients, a regional bank, is responsible for building a web-based application to give homeowners a mortgage quote. The bank was recently preparing to visit a potential mortgage customer, Margaret. What should the design team want to know about Margaret's context when using this application?

- **Process stage:** Where is Margaret in the process of applying for mortgages? Is she just starting out or has she already applied for several? Is she already a customer of the bank? What does she know about the bank? What does she need to know to make a decision?

- **Level of understanding:** Is this her first time purchasing a house? Does she understand how mortgages work? Is she clear on the differences between the various options?

- **Stage of purchase decision:** Has she chosen the house she wants to buy? If not, does she know the price range she can afford?

- **Motivation:** Why is she getting a quote? Does she want to know if she can afford her dream house? Does she want to compare rates with other lending institutions?

- **Next steps:** After she gets the quote, what will she do with the information? Is she likely to apply for the mortgage right away? Does she need to speak with others first? Who else will she talk to? Her husband? Her parents? Her realtor? What information will she want to share with them?

- **Previous knowledge:** What other online applications does she use regularly? Is she familiar with spreadsheets? Email? Word processors?

- **Tech-savviness:** Does Margaret do her banking online? Does she use online bill payment?

The list of questions the team put together was much longer than this, but you get the idea. Every question looked at a piece of Margaret's context. Every answer could have an impact on the design the team put together.

Following is a method for organizing these elements so we can think about them more easily:

- **Goals:** What is the user trying to accomplish? How do the user's actions fit into the objectives of the organization?

- **Process:** What steps will the user follow? How does information flow from one step to the next? What are the various roles (such as creator, contributor, editor, or approver) that are involved?

- **Inputs and outputs:** What materials and information will users need to successfully use the interface? What will they need from the interface to continue with their overarching goals?

- **Experience:** What similar things has the user done in the past? How has the organization survived without this design in the past?

- **Constraints:** What physical, temporal, or financial constraints are likely to impose themselves on the user's work?

- **Physical environment:** How much room do the users have to work? What materials are on their desks? What access do they have to necessary information (such as user manuals)? What is taped to their monitor?

- **Tools in use:** What hardware and software does the user currently use?

- **Relationships:** What are the interconnections between the primary user and other people who are affected by the tool?

By breaking down context into these components, we can organize our questions and be sure we've covered all the important issues. (That said, every project has a slightly different breakdown.)

Playing the guessing game

Before Jared and the UIE team go out on a field study, they like to play a game. They convert each of the above categories into a couple of questions, much like the questions about Margaret, the home buyer. For example, *inputs* becomes, "What personal information does the user need to apply for the mortgage?" and "Will the user have all the information at her fingertips when she starts the application process?"

Then, right before the first field visit, they use what they know about the person they're visiting to guess at the answers. Even though these are just guesses, they make an honest attempt to think through each answer, often discussing them among themselves. This process creates a painting in their heads, as it were, of who the user is and what they expect her context to be.

When they visit the user's site, any differences they see between the user's real environment and the painting in their heads jumps right out at them. It becomes easy to collect the data UIE needs during the visit.

Why not just brainstorm all the possible contextual elements, skip the visits altogether, and ensure the design meets every possible need? First, unless you're extremely lucky, your team won't have the resources to build a design that can accommodate every possible combination of contextual elements. Second, every field study discovers things the team could never have predicted, because the factors behind the context are different from the team's own experiences.

By observing how your potential users interact in their environment, you'll have a sense as to which contextual elements are most common and which ones can have the biggest impact on the usability of the design. Plus, you may see something that you never imagined could happen.

Design happens at the intersection of the user, the interface, and the user's context. It's essential for interface designers to understand the entire gamut of possible contexts, thereby ensuring they create designs that are usable no matter what's happening around the user.

It is through this understanding of a user's context that we can intelligently choose which frameworks to use and which design patterns to include with the implementation of each one.

In our fictional travel-site client's case, the users can have a variety of contexts. They might be organizing a business trip from the office, collecting ideas for a family vacation with kids in tow while at home, planning a weekend getaway with friends over drinks at a bar, or something else. Users will not, however, need to gain approval for travel plans here, because the resulting guide will only offer *recommendations*—not reservation options. In each of these cases, people are likely to use the site only long enough to get some quick recommendations before moving on. This is, basically, a *single-task site*. And on single-task sites, the best place for the starting point to the main task flow is usually front and center. The goal is to get ancillary functionality and information out of the way while still providing access to it, and let users rip through main the process at will.

Ah—the beginnings of the information architecture.

Beyond this, though, users need to be able to learn who is behind the site to know whether its recommendations are worthy of their attention and trust. *About Us*. To influence which recommendations appear in the resulting travel guide, users need a way to set site-wide preferences; for example, a user who takes business trips most of the time will quickly become annoyed at being forced to supply the same answers on repeat visits, so users should be allowed to specify default settings. *Account Management*. Users also need to find information on specific hotels, hot spots, gyms, and other things. *Search*. And of course, they need to be persuaded to use the site in the first place. *Sign-up*.

You're already up to four frameworks without yet having a single idea about the site's core task flow. You can start these things while you hash out with the client the details of the main draw: the customized, dynamic guide.

Much like an essay, choosing frameworks is a matter of breaking the project down into chunks and filling up those chunks with the details that bring them to life. In this section, we'll use A. In this one, B. Here, C. Then you piece it all together, write beautiful segues, fine-tune, and turn the sucker in. Instant website.

Of course, for those proverbial segues to be beautiful, you need to sort out how each site element will be presented. This is where design patterns and design criteria came into play.

Picking patterns

Because there is a lot of work to do when planning a trip and we don't want to waste a user's time, it's vital to create a streamlined task flow that moves users from A to Z without any meandering. Looking over the list of frameworks, you can start to make design decisions that support this notion. In a few days, you'll have a single-task site that includes the following:

- About Us
- Account management
- Search
- Sign-up

Because this is a single-task site that creates almost no risk for users—they won't purchase anything here, and they can freely choose to ignore the recommendations—the About Us section can be quite small. A little information about the people behind the recommendations and some quotes from the media will do just fine. And because this information is ancillary at best, the entry points to About Us can be tucked away in the corner of the navigation. Accessible, but out of the way. One decision down.

Account management need not be any more complicated than offering the user a simple form to specify trip preferences. Of course, account management includes several other essentials—a sign-in link, a sign-in form, a lost-password option, a sign-out link, a form for changing a password and updating the user's email address, and perhaps a reset-password page, depending on how you handle the lost-password process. These things are all standard: you've designed them many times before, and you have a set of recommendations on hand for the design of these elements. You're done thinking about this.

Search is a bit trickier, because, well, search is always tricky. For this site, you mainly have uniquely-identified content—hotels, restaurants, bars, and so on. Easy enough. But you also have a single-task site where you want the user to glide through the core task flow and use search only for horizontal exploration. That is, you want people to use search while in the middle of the the process of creating a guide, but you need them to get back to the guide as though it had never been interrupted. Further, you want them to add things from the search results to the guide, thereby customizing the guide and providing more value to the user. So, for this search system, you decide to stick the Search field only on the pages related to creating a guide (thereby excluding the About Us pages, for example), and include in the results pages an option to add a result to the user's travel guide.

One more context consideration. Once users put together a guide full of recommendations, you wonder, how will they keep the information on hand during the trip? They may have already booked the hotel, but do you expect them to memorize the locations of gyms, bars, restaurants, and events during the trip? Do you expect them to copy the information into some other document and consult it before leaving the hotel? The second context is that of this newly enlightened person wandering around an unfamiliar city struggling to recall the name and address of that hip, downtown bar the site recommended.

In addition to a streamlined task flow, you need to deliver a guide that can be used on the go. Users, you imagine, will want to email the guide to themselves or someone else, and they'll want to print it so they can carry it around in a pocket or purse during the trip, ready for quick reference.

Not particularly revolutionary, but much to your surprise, it is something no other travel guide site you know about has done. Suddenly, simply by understanding the user's context, you have a competitive differentiator (albeit one that's easy to copy).

Quite clever, you.

Applying design criteria

There is one aspect you haven't yet thought about: the sign-up framework.

Convincing users of the value of the application may be a simple matter of spelling it out on the home page (which, in this case, will be the starting point for every interaction a user has with the site), but because this is a site most users will traverse quickly, the method for setting up an account to maintain personal preferences needs to be entirely *frictionless*. A lengthy registration form here will kill any chance of conversion from visitor to repeat customer. In other words, you can't use a traditional registration form. In this case you need to handle registration in a new way. You check out the list of design criteria for the sign-up framework. One of these criteria gets you thinking: *Associate the user to the user's actions.*

Ideally, users won't need to do anything at all beyond what they came to do. They should simply be able to step through the core task flow, get the resulting travel guide, and be on their way. But when they come back at a future date, you want to have recorded their preferences somehow so you can make the process even easier.

To handle this, you decide to simply store the information a user enters upon first use and default to it next time. You also decide to ask somewhere along the task flow if the user wants to save the entered information as her default guide settings. The solution breaks away from the standard registration method, but in doing so, it increases the value of the site for repeat users. And by removing the barrier of the registration form, the site's usability actually *improves*.

You have a quick chat with the client to present your ideas, hash out a few details, and just like that, the design is in progress.

Nice work.

Making Frameworks Practical

You move to creating wireframes. Here is where pattern libraries begin to do their job.

Libraries

Inside a design firm where there are teams of designers at work on sites for a wide range of clients, framework and pattern libraries are pure gold. And inside an organization that spends all its time on its own sites, *component libraries* are invaluable. These resources help in planning, storyboarding, holding whiteboard sessions, prototyping, and experimenting by offering a shared tool set and a shared language of interface solutions that can be used and reused at the start of every project. If you are in one of these organizations, we highly recommend you create a framework and pattern library to correspond with your products to flesh out your reuse strategy.

But what happens when you get down to the level of the individual designer? When a designer actually needs to put these things onto a screen and turn them into something real—whether at a firm, at a Fortune 500 company, or operating as a lone consultant—how do you make patterns practical?

Well, there are a couple of answers.

First, you can strip down what's required for your library documentation. Instead of creating a full-fledged framework library, you can start the same way Robert did—by using his 37-Signals' Backpack account to create a page for each framework. As frameworks came up during projects, he simply started a new Writeboard page in Backpack, wrote up descriptions in each of the major sections, linked to examples of the patterns in public pattern libraries or cross-referenced his own stencils in OmniGraffle and other tools (see the next section for more about this), and wrote a list of design criteria. Over time, he built up his personal library (**Figure 9.1**) enough that he could simply write a list of frameworks to use at the beginning of a project and start putting designs together.

Second, you can work with stencils.

Figure 9.1
A list of frameworks from Robert's personal framework library

Stencils

While we were writing this book, one of the most pragmatic questions to come up as a result of Robert's framework workshops, sessions, and discussions was from someone who wanted to know why an individual designer—one not working with a team—needs his own framework or pattern library.

The answer is a bit tricky.

We don't deny that launching and curating a library is an arduous task. It's a safe bet that most solo designers have nowhere near the amount of time they need to create them. And even when a designer is part of a team, inside of a company, he still needs a way to make these resources practical, so that they *actually help him put screens together.*

To this, we ask: you know those tedious contact forms you have to design over and over again? And sign-in screens? And lost-password interactions? And tab interfaces? It can be extremely helpful for you to maintain a collection of these elements, in whatever tool you use for wireframes or composites, as reusable patterns. Enter *stencils.*

Figure 9.2
The stencils offered through the Yahoo Design Pattern Library include reusable pattern stencils for everything from web forms to Apple iPhone interfaces, from banner ads to page grids.

For example, Robert uses OmniGraffle for wireframes, a tool for which loads of people have created custom stencils. He uses these stencils to eliminate the need to recreate these elements all the time.

Basically, you can create a stencil that has nothing in it but your versions of common forms—sign-up, sign-in, contact, and so on, complete with error-handling designs that show appropriate error messaging. Whenever you need one of these forms, you can simply drag it out and tweak it rather than starting from scratch. Patterns thus become not only helpful in planning an application, they also become drag-and-drop solutions for creating actual screens.

As a designer, if you have previously dealt with the challenges of form design, it's likely you recommend the same types of solutions often; you probably handle error messages, layout, required fields, and so on, in similar ways each time. *These are your patterns. This is your library.* You don't need to write up all the details unless you need to share them with other team members, but you should most definitely turn your patterns into stencils that you can reuse and modify as needed. This takes a little time, but it takes significantly less time than creating these things from scratch on every project.

Every design tool you can use on a project supports reusability in some way. In high-end graphics tools, such as Adobe Photoshop, you can copy the layers for a search interface design into a new image document, save it, and copy it back into other designs later on. In wireframing tools, such as OmniGraffle and Microsoft Visio, you can create stencils filled with your patterns. In lower-end options, such as Apple Keynote and Microsoft PowerPoint, you can create slide decks that contain your custom shapes and such, and simply copy them into new designs.

Saving time on these rote elements will make that work less tedious, and will leave you ample time to focus on the more interesting and compelling aspects of a project.

With these resources on hand, all you have left to do is piece together the wireframes for the sections of the site that include these frameworks, hand them to the visual designer as they are completed, fine-tune the final pages as the developer builds them out, and spend the rest of your time focusing on the main task flow.

The thing your client really cares about.

The thing *you* really care about.

Improving the Future

When we started writing this book, we intended to present a simple introduction to frameworks along with an in-depth discussion of a catalog's worth of common examples. As we talked about frameworks at sessions and workshops over a period of months, however, we realized two important things.

First, the questions we were repeatedly asked about frameworks needed to be addressed in the book. Second, by giving you a catalog of completed frameworks, we would essentially be giving you a fish instead of teaching you *how* to fish. It's far more important that you learn how to think about, identify, and use frameworks on your own. To think about them critically. To learn to deconstruct the web from an anatomical perspective and apply the insights gained from doing so. As such, we revamped the scope and structure of the book into what you now hold in your hands. We believe it's a better book, and that it will be far more beneficial to you in the long run than what we originally intended.

To do this, we identified several goals.

We set out first to take a close look at what Rolf Molich referred to as "building blocks." Again, we believe frameworks, used in conjunction with design patterns and components, are what Rolf was hoping to see one day; frameworks offer a way to create more usable interfaces right out of the gate so you can rely less on usability testing and evaluation. In *Web Anatomy*, we strove to help you not only identify these building blocks, but also deconstruct and analyze them.

Next, we set out to help you better translate fuzzy project requirements into usable designs. We've seen countless projects go horribly awry as a result of the poor translation of weak specifications, and part of the reason we've done so much to advocate frameworks is to solve this exact problem.

We also set out to do something we believe design patterns cannot do—offer inspiration and a path to innovation. We did this by using frameworks as a way to reverse-engineer what other organizations have learned about human behavior, and build on their successes by extrapolating a list of design criteria for each framework. This list can then be used to devise innovative solutions that maintain a high degree of usability.

Finally, and perhaps most important, we aimed to guide you toward a more complete reuse strategy. Patterns and components are essential tools when teams are expected to do much with little, but patterns and components simply don't go far enough. Frameworks put these solutions in context. They offer a guideline for the design of complete user contexts and task flows. As such, they make for a more stable reuse strategy. Instead of jumping straight from the conceptual level of a design project to the nitty-gritty details of a design pattern or component, you can use frameworks to bridge the gap, ensuring your designs include the right solutions in the first place.

These may be lofty goals, but we strongly believe frameworks address all of them in an approachable and effective manner. To demonstrate this concept, however, we had to do some work. In this book, we looked at patterns and components in some depth, and then dove into frameworks—what they are, how to think about them, what they look like; how to write them, pull design criteria out of them, and apply those criteria; how to curate and share them, make them practical for your work, and choose source sites both in and out of your industry by which to validate them; and finally, how to put them to work in a hypothetical case study.

Beyond this, we've discussed what to consider when implementing your own designs. What makes them persuasive. What makes them usable. How context affects your design decisions.

We created as useful a book as we could, and we certainly hope you agree that it is as thorough a resource as the subject requires.

There is, however, one thing we haven't yet discussed: how to convince the check writers in your organization that the effort of developing frameworks and a framework library is worth it. We get this question quite a bit, actually—people constantly struggle to find ways to earn buy-in for design efforts—and we know that information about how to do this will be critical to your efforts later on. To build a better future, we must first understand the problems of the present.

A great way to demonstrate those problems is to measure the *cost of frustration*.

The Cost of Frustration

It's difficult to find someone who doesn't believe it's beneficial to make a more usable design, but it's also often quite difficult to justify the expense of design efforts and usability evaluations against other business priorities.

Poor design creates friction, and friction can manifest itself in countless ways. A shopper may abandon a sale. Company staff may spend more time than necessary dealing with critical information. The less the design jibes with what a user is trying to accomplish, the more friction increases.

When friction occurs, frustration comes next. Users may feel frustration because they can't complete their tasks. Employers may become frustrated because their employees are taking too long to perform critical functions.

A poor design results in high friction. High friction results in high frustration.

While it's often difficult to measure whether a design is poor or not, you can easily measure when frustration occurs. With a little digging, you can usually associate a dollar cost to the frustration, thereby giving you a way to estimate, in financial terms, the cost of the poor design.

Frustration usually shows up in one of four ways:

- Increased expenses

- Lost revenues

- Lost productivity

- Wasted development time

A problem that forces users to call the organization's toll-free number, for example, increases the number of required call-center operators. Similarly, an overly complex intranet design can make employees waste work time completing what should be simple information-gathering tasks.

Each organization feels frustration through a monetary impact. You can measure the monetary impact of handling a support call by dividing the support budget for a year by the number of calls handled.

When you estimate how many calls are related to a particular problem, you can use the cost-per-average-call to estimate the cost of handling the problem. Since you can easily tell if an alternative design produces less frustration, you can then estimate the cost difference, giving you a big piece of the return-on-investment puzzle.

Amtrak.com's cost of frustration

As an example, let's look at Amtrak.com, the official website for America's passenger railroad system, which UIE studied in 2004.

(Note: numbers in the following description are fictitious.)

Amtrak.com allows customers to make reservations online. Imagine we've observed during usability testing that the site makes it difficult to complete a registration. Only one out of every four attempts to book a registration online actually succeeds.

A quick analysis of the site's logs showed that the average reservation is for $220. It also showed that there were 10,000 reservations successfully completed every month, producing a monthly revenue stream of $2.2 million.

Inspection of the site's logs showed the same patterns we've seen in UIE's labs: only 25 percent of the people who started reservations actually completed them. That meant that 30,000 reservations per month went uncompleted. Using our average reservation cost, that puts the number of failed registrations at roughly $6.6 million per month, or $79.2 million a year.

That's a lot of money for Amtrak to recapture. However, many of those folks won't actually register, even if the site was much more usable. The design forced a potential traveler to start the registration process just to see what a fare cost or when trains run between two cities. Many of these travelers went for cheaper or more convenient travel and never registered.

Therefore, we needed to estimate our frustration cost carefully, removing these "no-go" users from our estimates. However, we found it difficult to accurately predict the percentage of visitors without knowing their purchase intentions. In this case, we'll conservatively estimate that only 20 percent of people who didn't register would have done so with an easier-to-use interface. (By estimating conservatively, we made it easier for others to put faith in our calculations, while also allowing for the happy surprise of exceeding our goals.)

Twenty percent of our 30,000 uncompleted registrations a month is 6,000 people who we think will register with an improved interface. That means that a well-designed reservation system could increase revenues by $1.32 million a month, or $15.84 million a year.

That means that we calculated the *cost of frustration* for Amtrak.com at almost $16 million annually.

Calculations like that ought to get someone's attention.

Practical calculations

To calculate Amtrak's cost of frustration, we needed to combine our usability testing results with company financial activity and website log files. The more data sources we used, the more solid our numbers became.

When we believe that the frustration results in lost revenue, we'll often look to identify the problems that get in the way of sales. However, we need to change how we calculate the costs for non-revenue types of frustration costs:

Increased expenses

We look at all the costs that the organization incurs because of the problem. These can be extra support calls, replacement materials, and increased server load.

Lost productivity

This is slightly more difficult to estimate. Ideally, you could take the annual cost of the affected employees and divide it by the number of hours they work per year. That would give you a cost-per-hour for a productive employee. Multiply that by the number of unproductive hours per year, and you have an annual productivity-loss figure.

However, it's sometimes hard to calculate the cost of the affected employees. Figuring out people's salaries, benefits, and other costs (such as the electricity they use) can be time-consuming and politically difficult. Sometimes it's easier for us if we talk about what those employees would do instead of dealing with the productivity loss. If we can talk about how salespeople would have 15 percent more time selling, we can often frame the frustration costs in terms of gains in the more productive activities.

Wasted development time

In many of today's software products and websites, there are entire areas of functionality that users never see or use. (One only needs to pull down the menus in a word processor to see the vast quantity of items rarely explored.) Developing these features and functions takes time, yet if no one knows they are there, what benefit is the publisher getting?

Looking at the list of features planned for development, we can see how much each one will cost to develop (using similar calculations to those we used for lost productivity). Relatively simple usability tests can help us identify if users can discover thefeatures and whether or not they'll use them once they've discovered them. In other words, we can calculate the costs developers waste building things that people won't use.

Looking for pain

With all this in mind, it may still be difficult to burst into the CEO's office and declare you can save the corporation millions of dollars with solid usability work, even though you've carefully calculated your cost of frustration. Instead, you need to go to the next best place: the source of the pain.

Usually, in an organization, where there is frustration, there is pain. Somebody is not getting what they want. If the website is so unusable that it stops shoppers in their tracks, then the sales and marketing people aren't making their numbers. If the support phones ring too often, the support-center manager has a staffing problem.

By following the pain to its source, you can often find important allies who may even have the budget to fund the usability work. At a minimum, having one more champion on your side is extremely beneficial.

Leveraging the cost of frustration

Assessing the cost of frustration is one of UIE's favorite ways to demonstrate the value of its work. If the team can pinpoint how frustrating the interfaces are and how that frustration is influencing the business, it becomes very easy to convince stakeholders they need to change their designs.

UIE's team members found once they start focusing on the underlying cost of frustration figures, they end up with an effective metric they can use throughout the development process. It helps them identify which designs are most effective and gives them a tool to explain the benefits of good design.

We hope this approach helps you as well.

Resources

To wrap up, we offer you a collection of resources on patterns, components, and frameworks. While we *fully* expect you to keep this book readily available at all times, every single day, within arm's reach of your desk, we understand you may benefit from additional resources. Following is a list we think will help you get started and build support for frameworks in your work.

- *Web Anatomy: Introducing Interaction Design Frameworks:* Robert's introductory article, which he wrote for UIE.com, can help you summarize the concept of frameworks and how they benefit designers. It's at http://www.uie.com/articles/web_anatomy_frameworks/.

- *Web Anatomy: Effective Interaction Design with Frameworks:* Robert's Virtual Seminar on frameworks is ninety minutes long and offers an introduction to frameworks followed by a Q&A session from attendees.

- *Spoolcast: Interaction Design Frameworks Seminar Q&A Follow-up:* Robert answers additional questions that came directly from attendees of his aforementioned Virtual Seminar about frameworks. It's at http://www.uie.com/brainsparks/2009/06/03/spoolcast-interaction-design-frameworks-seminar-qa-follow-up/.

And, of course, you have access to perhaps the most valuable resource of all, the first publicly available framework library, available at http://webanatomy.rhjr.net.

If you have questions beyond what these resources offer, you can contact Robert Hoekman, Jr, through his personal website at www.rhjr.net, or Jared Spool through his company's website at www.uie.com.

Index